CONVERSATIONS

Selected poems

Toni K Williams

Art work by Jami Tobey Kiendra

Used by permission.

Dedication

Three stars light my way without requiring explanations.

Christopher, Jami, Joshua

Love you forever, Mom

Acknowledgements

My deepest appreciation for the gifts of women who forever uplift and cheer me on with elbow nudges and mirth. You fill my lap with quirky color and so it was on a winter day after another elbow nudge. OUCH, I began gathering my bits and pieces and dressed my shrugging it off, and fluttering words in book form. Gratitude, applause, and a thousand printed Thanks is simply not a large enough expression.

Thank you, Jami, for permission to use your incredible paintings. Your lovely spirit is a gift. Karen, without complaint, you cast a wise eye across these pages, regularly penciling in, "wow, nope, what is this word? use hyphens; what are you trying to say, and no one knows this word, it's ancient." You kept the boat floating with all sorts of interesting finds and daily changes in poem order. Daily! Carolyn, you are always steady and patient on the tiller, completely serene in storm or calm. When I grow up, I would like to be like you. Marilyn. Always!

I Seedlings

The time has come
the Walrus said, to talk of many things:
Of shoes and ships and sealing wax,
of cabbages and kings.

Lewis Carroll

I Seedlings

VIGNETTE I

What did you ever learn

Once upon a child's time ago

When the sun could shine a cloud away

And roses meant red?

Do you recall?

Clouds were elephants.

THE SILENT WAIT

Amber light bathing
This cradle of ideas rocking
Liquid
Anticipation electric
The silent wait
Expecting to soar
Infinity
Galaxies divinity
Plucking stars
From the endless
Creations of God.
I will put the brightest
In paper sacks
And bring them home
To light my Mother's eyes
With dandelions.

I am the silent wait
Quiet coiled
A small seed of
Yet To Be
Soft
Swaying
Tucked
In spinning limbo
Holding the arch of time
In a fist
Waiting for
Amen.

SNOW

Snow is doomed.
Children know this.
Winter can't last.
But when it happened
Wind came at night.
Opening shades we could see
Jack Frost messages on cold glass.
No sound in a world
Gone the color of white sheets.
Oh! to be suddenly
Alone
Out there.

We slipped and fell on our way to school
In slick halls we skidded
Sliding happy
Ice melting from mittens
Chattering excitement
We can always hope for more snow.

Cold feet red-toed
Cheeks glowing rosy iced
Fingers and lips chapped
Cold pinching ears
We closed our eyes and listened
Winter
Then snow fell again.
For days.

SUMMER NIGHTS

Summer nights called me
Awake
Hearing dogs bark
At cats next door.
My sister sleeps tight
In her bed across the room
Dreaming heavy.
I tiptoe soft into night
Pink nightgown fluttering
In light from backyard breezes
My father in the yard
Bends
Bordered
By the smell of
Cut grass
Pant cuffs hose soaked from watering.
I creep quiet outside
Watch his dark outline
Large
Bowed over
Tending plants.
He turns
Brushing his hands together
Knowing I am standing there
Waiting to breathe.
Let's go walking he says
We can plan what comes next.
Down the sidewalk we go
In the dark
Me skipping
He striding
His hand helping me
Think things over.
I climb
Between cotton sheets
When darkness turns cool
His kiss dries on my forehead.

FOR BRUCE

We saw his dying
The motorcycle flying
Lying heaped
He was spinning
As lightly as
Feather
Forever
Then kissed death
On the pavement shoulder
Perhaps he is spinning still
Through galaxies

Grouped around the shrine
Of bloodied gravel

       Crying
       Sobbing
       Why. Why! WHY?

Thank God, it wasn't me...
We are all selfish with death you know.

We prayed silent.
Mostly for ourselves
Because at seventeen
We were all immortal
Summer suns had scarcely
Browned us.

We all grew up
That hot June day
When life drew back
A fearsome curtain
Bidding us gape and gasp
Our future possibilities.

It seemed a sadistic joke
For him to lose the race
Before it was fairly begun
Hasn't Death ever heard
Of sportsmanship?

HIGH SCHOOL BOYFRIENDS

Even after all these years
I am startled occasionally
Awake
By your face
Pressing in on
The silk of my sleep.

You never understood
Or tried to be my friend.
Your biggest contribution
To my life
Was embarrassment.
You could have asked me
To the Junior Prom.

THE HERO OF MY COLLEGE DAYS

Remembering
Will always be
The only taste
Of your infinity.
Remembering will speckle me
With all the dusty, ashen
Probabilities
That ever were
And never were
And never had a chance to be.
In all the trembling
Static nights
To come
When all the dreamer's
Opportunities
All the silvered crystal
Possibilities
Abruptly end
In cracked and broken actualities
I will be remembering.

GRANDMOTHER'S CHAIR

Her armchair needs recovered
Horsehair stuffing
Escapes through tiny holes
Splitting thread bare
Dull gold brocade
Rending ruin
We can scarcely see the pattern
Anymore.
Her chair endures creeping clutter
Drifting to the floor
Faded
Stained
From too much use
Unworthy of living rooms
Too many lingering lives
Too many naps
Too many goodbyes
Too many funeral griefs
Too many children
Climbing up and over jumping
Landing
Thump
Hard near fireplace bricks.

So many happy bodies flung
Sideways casual nested
My wild brown summer legs
Swinging loose over cushioned arms
Reading.
Wondering.
Daydreaming.

Grandmother's chair
Wrapped sturdy old arms
Around hugs of laughter

Shelved my curled tanned feet
Dirty on the bottom
From going forbidden barefoot
In early morning grass
Running toward fresh pastures
Where horses whinnied
Beckoning me on their backs.
That funny stain
Is mascara tears
I cried for you.

This lovely old relic
Welcomed adventures
Loved books.
Nancy Drew
Hardy Boys
Shakespeare's sonnets
The Yellow Wallpaper
Cask of Amontillado
Frost, Eliot, Tennyson.
Her chair
Protected love letters
Intricate careful conversations
Tearful upsets
Dear ones
Fat dreams
Lonely heartaches
And once your stretched-out smile
As you sprawled
Laughing.

I dismiss appeals for new fabric
Covering remains of my ancient stories
Resting for a spell.

Re. Up. Holstered?
How could it be the same refuge?
Wrapped in shabby dignity
Her chair reminds me of my heart.

WILL'S TRUCK

When I think of him
I scarcely see his face.
If I concentrate
His eyes visit me
Commanded by joyous collections
This child's heart shouts out loud.

All these years later
I see his back
Straight and strong
Easily in rhythm with his horse.
This man once turned a
Wild headlong stampede
Rushing panicked cliff edged frantic
Along the Weber River
Saving herd and cowboys.

Seizing heart pictures
My sense of smell takes over
Levi jacket, barn boots
Horse sweat and leather
Sagebrush, cowboy coffee
Mud, shovels, lariats
Saddles, jingling bridles
Bumping across sandy red earth
Counting moaning cows
Searching for bawling calves.
Early sunrise yawning
Leaning on his shoulder.
Summer sky blue infinity
His gaze clear
Wraps my day in sunshine.

I think of him
With eyes closed behind sunglasses

Longing for the jolting bounce
His aging banged-up truck
Faltering springs squealing
Gathers leaping children
Laughing
Smells like wet dog Old Bob.
Sanctuary.
Hay bales, grain sacks
Oil, rust
Cracked seats
Broken windshield
Floor shift three-speed
Protesting Chevy pick-up truck
Granny gear groaning.
His voice amused
Words hugging me
It is the nicest piece
Of remembering I own.

THE FARM

Long shadows split the valley
Marking evening with dark notches
Along fields of new-cut hay
Thresher's dust hangs yellow
Covering evening rustling
Scrub oak's rusty color
Slides Autumn down hillsides.
Sunset sings lingering ballads
Sending swords of last light
Stalking the end of day.
A red-winged black bird
Comes roosting home calling
On the fringed cradle of cattails

TENDING CALVES

I thought of you today
Grandpa
Tending white-faced
Hereford calves
Butting heads across
Springtime pastures
Beside the haystack.
Near the fence
Two black dark-eyed
Suffolk lambs buck
Bleating at the trough edge
A mother ewe fatly wooled
Guards carefully.

Everywhere earth dresses spring
Wears budding bright leaf scarves.
Daffodils shine yellow crown nods
Parading corners of the farm road.
Pastures celebrate
Lavish brazen growing things
Broadcasting spring jubilees.
"Wake up I am here
Evicting winter."

Clouds thick fleeced as sheep
Wander lazy rambles
Transversing a buttery morning
Silky blushing pink bouquets
Hold waking promises.

I missed you today Grandpa.
Twelve years gone
Beneath the earth
Yet so close
I touched your smile on my cheek
Your pat on my knee

You whistling the dog
White butterflies flutter recalls
Tasting like wildflowers
Celebrating.
The flavor of cold well water
Summer wet glides across my tongue.

On my road today
Spring brings applause
In loud hallelujahs.

GREATMOTHER'S HANDS

She appears in dreams.
Her white hands elegant with rings.
Her white hands carry a thousand sorrows
Lift a thousand wishes
To her breast.
Her white hands with long lotus fingers
The little one bent at the middle joint
Just like mine.

Her white hands stroke fevered brows
Comb tangled hair
Hem petticoats, mend catastrophes
Large and small.
Her touch burns lives with hope.
Her white hands
Wrist deep in the work of winter
Carry baskets of burdens with grace
Washing small bodies
Convincing larger ones
Coaxing babies into the world
With pain between her thighs

Her white hands stir kettles
Thick with steam
Across kitchen sounds of children
Her white hands peel vegetables
Pick peaches and plums from fall trees
Turn to bandage wounds looking for the lost.

Her white hands spin air with laughter
Polish tables, clean knives with lemon,
Soak laundry
Pause at sunset
Shading weary topaz eyes
She gifts us wise.

Her white hands soar above our family world
Her embrace a dove's wing
Holding us composed
Overtakes the stuttering flight of
Our soul fears
Pours out diamonds of comfort
Drying cheeks after the overflow of nightmares.

Her white hands with long lotus fingers
Clutch knuckle-pale the satin edge of coffins.
Stroking frosty cheeks of doomed sons
She whispers soft mother words
Sending them across stars before her.

Her white hands choke sorrow sighs
Dry tears
Kiss goodbyes
Gather calm in her warrior lap
Rock sleepy newborns in cradles.
Babies fat with dream stories
Float drowsy on sounds of her harp voice
Lullabying honey in the night.

Her white hands elegant with rings
Wrap orange and purple silks around her hips.
Willful, stubborn against grief
She plucks up threads of
Patience
Dancing, whirling, spinning, singing
Her white hands begin again
Weaving the humming sound of
Future generations.

SUICIDE

They called the night Francis
Shot herself
Straight through the soft pallet
Of her mouth.

I was eight months pregnant
Swollen with new life
Impatient
Waiting
Belly skin jumping
Rippling knocking.
A keen migration of unborn wonder
Sharing my breath.

They called
The night Francis
Put a .32 in her mouth
And erotically
Pulled the trigger.

Her teeth flew
All over hell.
We picked them up
Throwing away her tangled state of mind.
It wasn't the grisly blood
Giving offense
It was picking up
All those pieces of teeth
One by One.

I remember disbelief.
Francis didn't die.
She simply left her sensational confusion
Smeared ceiling to floor

A dramatic shocking sticky mess
Someone else had to clean up.
I remember sorrow
Eight months pregnant
Scrubbing on my knees
A lovely impatient heartbeat
Leaping under my skin
Eager for life
Keeping me company.

CHILDBEARING

I was a girl first.
Before I shared my body
Before we broke it together
With your birthing
You leaping eagerly from my womb
Into the arms of your new life
While dying breathed silhouettes
I was a girl first
Who took a lover
To become
A mother.

OXYGEN

Pushing
Birthing
      Breathing
            Crying
Flesh pushing flesh of my flesh
High pitched
      Breathing
            Groaning
Mouth making an 0
Panting
      Breathing
            Only
Breathing past the pushing
Eyes
      Closed
            Pushing
Husband wide-eyed talking
Good
      Pushing
            Flesh

Flesh of my flesh
Gathering
      Up
            Strength
Bearing down breaking
Infant
      Shouts
            Oxygen
Flesh of my flesh
      Pushed to discovery.
            Tears gasp smiles.

One day I will push again.

Pushing my woman self
Between all the tiny spaces
In and out and in between.
I will push myself past
Flesh of my flesh
Past the wide old woman
I have become

      Pushing
           One
                Last
                    Breath

Through the body's final gate.

FOR MY CHILDREN

I feel the heaving
Of your coming
Slow numbing fire of pain
Searing upward to my beating heart
Breaking me fragile
Slivers of crystal sparkling
With the weight of your arrival.

Then holding you
Enfolding you
A part of me
Apart from me
A newer life to ride the earth
More skillfully I hope than me.
My ecstasy of joyous welcome singing
Transforms
Singing belongs to you now
Instead of me.

WARRIORS

Warriors come home from battles
Strutting scars
Flinging medals
Captured on their spear-tips.
Everyone gathers
To make a celebration
Applaud and feast them.

Warriors strip
Dancing in loincloths
Parading their proud
Naked virility
Like honored trophies.

II

Young mothers
Parade prodigious offspring
Performing gurgles and sighs
For the benefit of
Doting grandparents
And bored friends.

Babies are medals
Won in bloody battle
Unfortunately
Scars only show
When women are naked
And stand on their heads.
Where is the feast for us?
And who will dance
Our damaged femininity?

THE MOTHER SONG

What lake gowns
The symphony of woman's
Tiny goddess feet?
A flood of sun sky
Enormous
Music delirious
Soars above her diamond moan

She is rain
True and powerful
Watering the tempo
Of your growing

She sings the rings
Of heaven's ladder
Laughing
Down the sky
Shaking silvered water
From her hand
Blessing you

She shelters your languid
Honey notes
When her palm rests
On your knee

She is the lake of herself.

    And She is

        She in you.

ORPHANED

They called last night
And told me he is dead.
They told me he is
Dead.
Outside dry darkness on the patio
Sits still under stars of summer.
Orion's Belt freezes
His leaving minute
In starlight sent a billion years
A billion miles away
Millenniums ago.

Cloud banks lavender cluster
Spreading a sundown of
Desolation
Over Sandia mountains
Stained watermelon colors
Along the Rio Grande.
The moon's slanted eye
Hooks fragile light
Discovering fringes of
Cottonwood trees
Shares rivers of teardrops
Fleeing.

Aroused an owl hoots
Coyotes bark and yip
Outside the grape stake fence
Pinion trees spread
Dry desert perfume
Shaking castanet needles
Clacking in solemn orchestrations
That should have been a typhoon
The night sprinkler
Thumps water bent against
Bleached adobe walls.

In the house my son makes lamplit
Phone calls
Too young at any age for this sort of duty.
The house blurs.
I turn my face to the wall.
Across new darkness
My son calls
"Mom?"

They called last night.
Dad is over.
My breath fell bottomless
Between unknown solar systems
At the speed of light
Spreading the news.

In summers I heard
Home sounds of a sprinkler
Watering his back yard
Smelled mowed grass.
Dad moved in the rustle of night
Checking the growing things
Tending growing things
Talking to growing things
I am his growing thing.

They called last night
And told me he is dead.
Gone.
So this is what
An orphan is.

FOR MY FATHER

Who can write the sum of any man's life?
The additions and subtractions?
The divisions?
The multiplications?
The infinite numberings
Coloring and counting
All his living landscapes
Exquisite.
Who can write songs of a grin
Or music hallowed
In echoes of his whistle calling
Across acres of mountains?
Who can write the complexities of
thinking
And ecstasies of Being?
Who can write
The sum of any man's life?

He is Son and Brother
Lover and Husband
Father and Friend
Mentor and Competitor
Protector and Teacher
Laborer and Builder
Champion.

He is Whistler and Comedian
Soldier of sorrows
Singer of sonnets and lullabies
He is a Gardener of small things
Guardian of tiny children
He is wind-pulling his hair
Running down the street
Behind a wild child
On a wobbly bicycle
Letting go.

He is the tender Companion
Of the night and day
The shade tree of our intent.
He is the ardent Debater
Forever curious.
He is the arm of strength
His hand seizing us
By our hair
Pulling us always
From the undertow.
He is love.forever.

THE GRANDE DAMES

My mother, my aunt
Ride cozy in the backseat
Bound north for Pocatello, Idaho.
I am their chauffeur today
Holding them steady on the highway
Escorting their talkative outing.
Grande Dames in their late 80s
Have a lot of chatter.
These two lived all their days close
Together.
I call this sister union
Cradle to Grave.

Now they are ancient wood
Polished by sun and storm
Twined with age rings
The bark of their skin
Wrinkled, gnarly
Freckled with aged sun spots
Merrily laughing
Quarreling a bit
Still competing
Planning lunch.

Ears glitter with gold.
Calloused hands heavy with rings
Record long ago passions
Now ancient history
Decades long gone.
Ladies traveling a northern highway
Also travel heavenward
Scudding clouds in a midnight sky
Fleeing before the waning moon
Pushed by winds
Nearly a hundred seasons turning.

They are stacked
Against the odds of time
That old mountain
Gets in the way of all pioneers.
Their wise lives
Swollen with age
Weighty with wheelbarrows of insight
Learned in the school of Hard Knocks.

Living through wars
Marriage.
Childbearing.
Sweat. Work. Loss.
Hardship. Fear.
Worry. Hallelujahs. Companionship.
Loneliness.
Disappointment.
Abandonment.
Death.
And of course Love.

They are my precious passengers
Chatting.
Arguing.
Competing.
Unaware
Shriveling toward invisibility
In the fullness of time
And they are elegant.
Beautifully.
Skillfully.
Delightfully.
Ripe\
Too soon they will fall from the tree
Kindling for the great flame.

Watching
In the rear-view mirror
We are silly laughing
With bright autumn
Rocky Mountain passion
Driving a freeway of
Reminiscence
Enjoying bawdy jokes
Family legends
Tall tales generations old.

We are having an ordinary
Women of the West
Driving to Pocatello day.
Grand Dames
All jingly with jewelry
Rosy rouged in their get up
Going places.

WHEN THE CURTAIN COMES DOWN

Stage lights down
House lights up
We players move soundless
In a deficiency of speech
Scripted conversations
Posturing words once belonging to
Someone else banging out pages
Of wishes and demands
Sweating
In some far off quarter of a
Blood rushed world
So distant now
Only spelling allows contact.

We strike the set with hammers
Pack makeup boxes and costumes
Moving in trances away
From carefully crafted
Counterfeit intimacies.

Our lizard skins of make-believe
Are shed with heavy sighs
Folded in trunks
Locked away.
The set is struck.
Curtain closed.
Wardrobe packed.
Lights off.
Doors locked.
Darkness blanks the theatre
Closing night puts our lives
Back on pause.

We slide unevenly
Returning to closet shelves
Of ordinary customs
Until another character
Comes mesmerizing yearning
Flags us down
Beckoning
Calling
Seducing
With a tempting tune of
Oh costume up
Come play Let's Pretend
We actors
Are drained of everything
Except the need for applause.

Coming home takes hours
Maybe days
Sometimes weeks
Perhaps years
On the boards where illusions fool around
We become a faking crowd
Deciding momentary meaning
More significantly arty than
Talking over cereal
In the morning
In the kitchen
Where dishes stack
Laundry piles
Lawns wait for mowers
Weeds require pulling.

We players giggle in daydreams
Figments of nothing much
Dance tunes and miracles
Floating blue skies in
Disneyland.

Artifice is the thirst for art
Until the curtain rings down tomorrow
Where there are
No more
Meshed and merging moon-dark
False footprints or opinions
On paths of transitory relationships
Gone.

Home again
My love objects are arranged
Where I left them.
Some sprawl
Some are curled tight in their beds
One snores
They are beautifully wonderful
Waiting yawning morning conversations
Sleepers of mine.
If I die tomorrow
Where will all our talking go
When I need to find out who we are
Today?

JUDY'S BREAD

Sitting
In your warm blue kitchen
Sipping my long gone by
Cup of grief
These past years
I have ever so
Watchfully gardened and
Tenderly nourished
Since the time we were neighbors
Down a street of futures
On the night he never came back.
Stacked sorrows
Basket brought
Keenly itemized
On your kitchen table
      One.   By.   One.
Rehearsing memorized worn futilities
And woes
And failures
And eroding shame
And dead conversations
Worrying the old bones of
Long gone.
Singing a chorus of current affairs
      One.   By.   One.
Your heart
      With mine
            Craving forgiveness.
You knead bread dough.
Our conversation
Pours over my head
Warm as prophet's oil
Anointing-wise.
    "I'm glad for you"
        you said

Looking through blue curtained
Kitchen windows beyond fence posts
Pasturing cows and calves
A pile of separated chaff
Eave-high to the barn
Spills messy wind tossed
Harvest rubble
Gusting delirious delicious
Cartwheeling over spring wheat
Hurled skyborne.
You tumble away my dry and scaly
Mocking straw stacks
Chucking inconsequential
Winnowed life husks
Into the chipper.

In your kitchen
Bread bakes fresh smells
Begging honey butter.
Sorrows hard kept gnawing flee
My heart's stormy gusts
Smiling broad.

You take bread
Fresh
From your oven.
Bread.
The Staff of Life.
     "I made it"
          you said
               "With your grain."

YAQUINA HEAD

The light house lifts
Yaquina Head aloof
White.
Sun shadows carve
Sleek stark whitewash
Into angles
Above the rocks
Above the spray
Above our heads.
That light
You said
Could be seen twenty miles
Twenty miles!

Out to sea
Fleets of shrimpers
Orienting land
Finding dry land again.
Twenty inches from your hand
I empty my sea-dreaming net
Your fingers curl slack
No beam to find that coastline.

Hardy Boys play detective In
the shrimper's focsil.
The lighthouse beam
Spins out
Lurches in
Catching red spattered
Flares of blood
Peppering the ice
Jiggers Boys!

Purified
Consecrated
Light sweeps
Darkness out of the way
Beating flares of wave rhythms
Bowing across black waters
Thumping portholes
Silence dazzles.
Darkness returns
Churning seas beneath the keel
Tosses life drowning
Again

A sweeping knock brightness
Flares on the up and downing
Wave-rocked windows.
Gone.
Back.
Gone again.
The shout of light
Bends another shining burst
Across the sea-foam spray
Black.
White.
Light.
Dark.
Light.
Dark.
The Pacific swings up and down
Rocking ships
Rocking men on slippery decks.
Rocking shrimp boat mesh nets
Drifting sideways
Like my life
Drifting
Then the black is back
Waiting.

Jiggers Boys
The game is over
Let's go home.

Black-roofed
Sea-sided
Soaring
The light house floats
Above the tide line boom
Above a spit of jagged rock
Above our heads.
You were saying?
About the Hardy Boys
Playing catch in shrimp boats?

I'm sorry
I was concentrating
On the sandy toes of tennis shoes
Hearing the chant of words
Like monk's expressions
Hidden in hooded cowls
Watching the light house
Fix the point of
Certain land.

I wondered later
Would your mouth have tasted
Like Pacific salt.

THIS SPRING'S POEM

I arrive surprised landlocked
In Santa Fe
Absent wild green storm-tight tension
Pacific's rolling sighs now heavily
Out of view
Advancing tides heave unseen
Cross-grained to my center
My heart beats sizzling surprise.

I arrive landlocked
In Santa Fe
Sand and crooked cactus
Tall clouds climbing frontiers
Every booted step on the desert floor
Falls away dusty
Sending lizards scuttling
Over blistered rocks
Agitated.

Dogs bark in the backyard
Some spring bird startles.
I howl at the moon
This unknown spicy desert moon
Grown too bursting yellow big
For me to lift
Sits down on black mountains
Casts a close haunting
Through mottled poplar shadows
Stalking cactus in the backyard lawn.

On the flute tune of dryness
Spring rises in Santa Fe
Carrying strong seeds of buffalo grass
Flings a song tolling
Against the bones of pinon hills
Jutting hard-fisted into the fired sky.

In the Kiva
Proud burnt old men
Lean against
A thousand years
Of turquoise dreams
Chewing peyote
Setting loose the soul eaters
Against a savage sunset.

I arrive landlocked in spring
In Santa Fe
Teeth chattering.
Red rock bluffs
Push against the chest
Of some unnamed warrior Sky God
Spitting hulls
Of pinion nuts
Into the ceaseless pueblo wind.

GOD'S VOICE

In the desert God's voice calls
In harmonies of colored sand
Glowing rainbow painted vivid
Flashing against thunder skies.
In the desert I taste
God's mouth pouring sweet
Into this throat dryness
Aching for the truth of divinity.
I answer back
In prayer harmonies
Drumming against rumbling skies.

In the desert
I come calling God down
That light of heaven
Keeping mountains arched.
There is combustion in this desert sky
Singing Godsongs
Chorusing liquid soul flames
Burning river beds pure.

Walking over drought stones
Rolled round and round
Turned over and over
Slowly rounding
A thousand millenniums
Turning
Banging together
Changing places
Becoming quiet.

Behind my burned back
God croons to me with sighs
Watering my arid sagebrush
Desert fields
Green again.

God touches me
With tender wisdoms
Whispers
His sirocco breath baring skin
To the bone
On the bones of the earth
On the bones of this soul
He speaks languages steadfast
Getting to the heart of the matter.

Oh, lend me respect God.
Fill me with rain answers
Pelting the windshield.
Answers airborne smashing against glass.
Answers weightless in passages
Between red blood cells.
Rain me peace
Against this hardpan soil
Where there is famine.

CRUISIN'

We were cruisin' north to Taos
Along the Rio Grande
Top Down
Gettin Brown
"I Need a Hero" blastin'
On the radio as we race passin'
Red Car speedin flashin'
Curves ahead.

Big girls in jeaned silk panties
Playin down-shift games so fancy
On every canyon corner
Along the Rio Grande.
Wild ladies rockin'
Heads back laughin, talkin'
Rock 'n rollin singing very loud.

We were cruising north to Taos
To see the Chocolatier
Looking for some decadent delight
Full Moon
Guitar tuned
Friday night
Shirt tight
Boots on
Singin' songs
Waitin' for JJ Cale at the
Sagebrush Inn.

We stopped for some enchantment
In the sunset land of bandits
And the man behind the counter
Poured us cocoa in a cup.

Sip it up
Spit it up
Drink it up
Ladies it is on the house
We are sweatin' in our blouses
And little did we know
That mindless fool was dousin'
With a little drop of juice called
Ramp it Up.

In a minute we start prancin'
With the light posts ballroom dancin'
The blurry people glancin'
At us cruisin' on the city square.

Across the street at old La Fonda
DH Lawrence rooms with Wanda
Aldus Huxley's bangin' Georgia in the back.
Hair down
Downtown
Boots off
We're tossed
Still waitin' for JJ Cale at the Sagebrush Inn.

Then this cowboy comes along
Singin' old James Taylor songs
And we are lost as lost
Strange as we can be.
The thing about a cowboy
Who is their mamma's joy
Is not their lanky legs
Or the broken ribs you feel beneath their shirt.
A cowboy can say "ma'am"
Clear his throat and purr a "darlin'"
And a woman might just as well disrobe.

So this long-limbed leggy dude
With a smile shy yet lewd
Wants to dance with us
Beneath the Taos stars.
And we ladies swoon with visions
Of the miles we have driven
For a little piece of chocolate
In the afternoon.

ATMOSPHERIC PRESSURE

I want to ride the West Wind!
The mystery wind!
The burning wind scrubbing foam
Cresting Pacific whitecaps
Heating land swells in vapor
With the blast
Of his wide uncovered mouth
Streaming molten spit.

I want to ride the West Wind!
The enchanted wind!
The gale wind
Expanding sunset open
Racing fog ponies hot over
Sky dark trails
Sprinting before sparking stars
Opposing blackness
Applying light
Blinking surprise
At the ashen nothingness
Of Time.

I want to ride the West Wind!
The frenzied Wind!
The howling Wind!
Becoming cyclone's child
Body rushing open
Skin sea air wet
Leaning low wind galloping
Unaccountable
Free over high mountain chains
Flinging aside the western night
Holding up the moon.

I want to ride the West Wind\
The barking wind
Disordering hymns of relocation
Storms of laughter panting
Earth crying tears of tenderness
At the arrival of his steaming breath.

RETURNING NORTH

The heaviness of snow
Bends winter long grasses yellow
Broken prostrate stalks flattened.
Ice flees runoff rivers
Snow captive waters rebel
Smack scattered boulders
Drown stream beds
Deliver floods
Obey gravity commandments
Baptize new life in white water
Immersion turns away the dark season.
Green plants rise
Young, soft, incomplete
Hungry for sun
Surge urgent up in plowed fields.
Grow.
Thrive.
Yearn.
Swallowing light.

Geese return north
Trumpeting hellos and
Boisterous hallelujahs
"We made it."

Children with full baskets of noise
Rackety shout and scream discovery.
We raft rapid currents
Bobbing over fast water
Plucking at water ripples

Pointing at calves wobbling birth
Lambs suckling
Small things peeping from bushes.
We grow.
Thrive.
Yearn.
Swallowing light.

TUCKED IN

Warm campfire quiet
Horses nicker stamping hooves
The best dog in the world
Blinks at the camera curious
Granddaughter laughing
Tucks me in tight.
Only two weeks since the wreck
When light near early left my eyes
Exchanged for stars.

It is a mountain evening of
All evenings.
We breathe campfire smoke
Burning marshmallows
Pine, sage, wild lilies, sweet grass
Wet dog
Horse blanket sweat
Saddle leather
Smiles.
Close your eyes
Listen to the sound of slumber
Waiting in woods
Happy bodies slide giggling
Into sleeping bag cocoons.

Shall I tell you a secret?
You will find me centered where wind
Pushes trees hard somersaulting
Against mountain folds
Sweeps yellow pollen peppering
Scrub juniper
Follows elk trails to rivers
Mad with rapids
Tangles hair scruffy
Hides in canyon corners
Carving cliff caves
Drags ground cover
Digs trenches in cold water creeks
Where startled pink toes curl
And mud squeezes under fingernails.

When day says goodnight
Moonless shadows carry
Owl's feathered hush
Collapsing clouds glide silence
Unroll angels and dragons
Wandering west
Hunting.

Sun abandons dulled day
Icy rivers hurl the lost pace of time
Mumbling over smoothed rocks
With no edges.

Missing other horses and
Good dogs tonight
And always my children
Long ago shouting happy
Children taking my breath away
With everything wonderful in the world.

WINTER BEINGS

I fast approach the darkest day of the year
Being Good King Wenceslas in long johns
Wading snow drifts heavy
Carrying horse forage from the barn
Pushing snow forward on paths
Horses pasture stamped.
My little herd grown winter hairy
Nickers bold impatience.
Frosted muzzles snort
Misty clouds of steam
Cold faces press eager
Over corral rails.
Blue dog swaggers
Darting checkpoints for invaders
Jumping fence high
Patrolling boundaries
His outside duty.

We winter beings
Breathe steam together
Freeze eyebrows
Wipe runny noses
Pull a hat over ears
Pat silky whiskered nuzzling noses
Hooves form ice balls
Snow-covered blue dog barks
Eager enthusiasms.
Hoar frost laces fence lines.

We huddle up
A gang of varied beings
Pressed together.
Horses shove pushing
Stretched necks greedy for
Buckets swollen with sweet corn
Warmth

Chuckling love
Bouncing laughter
Barks, snorts, squeals, sighs
High spirits rejoice in deepening
Cold.

Breath is winter
Icicles tinkle on manes
Blue dog pokes his nose in holes
Testing pasture oddities.
Snow-heavy pines surrender
The weight of snowpack
Hunching bent branches
Over waist-high drifts.
Another solstice twilight bleeds
The western sky
Marking evening in darkening degrees
Devoid of light.

The kitchen table
Waits with hot chocolate
Dressed in a worn old
Christmas tablecloth
I am fond of using
A collection from long ago befores.
On the back porch
Numbed feet kick-off
Toe pinching boots
Shedding parkas
Coming in the house brrrrr.

Tell me, love,
How did time slide away so invisible
Rewriting us along crooked decades
Arriving on arctic reminders tonight?
Only a threadbare treasured tablecloth
Celebrates once upon a time.

Night opens afterworld songs
Choiring red robed on western peaks.
Big Dipper's basket holds
Snow waltzing solstice hesitations
Steady
On the darkest day
Cold.

FAMILIES

We are neatly packed
And stacked
Tidily dusted
Arranged and resting
On the library shelf.
Only our paper covers
Rub together
Keeping everything inside
And out.
When did we ever open up
The volumes
Next to us
And read a chapter?
Pages swell
With our own dissembled poetry
Growing moldy
Over time.
We never look beyond
Another's title
And deem it worth
The reading.

VIGNETTE II

We have forgotten our stories

We have forgotten our names.

Thieves made off with our treasures

While we watched

Silent

Beside the ashes *of beacon fires*

As *day sank down*

Into the lap of

Night

II Saplings

How peaceful life would be without love.

How tranquil. How safe. How dull.

TKW

VIGNETTE III

I have loved

Twice

Double two

Which makes me

Either very wise

Or an incalculable

Fool

THE BIRTH OF VENUS

A girl needs a man
To make her a woman.
We can't quite grow-up
Until a man comes along
Introducing intimacies.
Ah, now we begin to
Understand.

A man needs a woman
In his fear of
Being alone
In the night.
And to help him prove
The force of his virility.
A woman gives him confidence
To go on
Being a man in the morning.

A woman needs a man
In her fear of
Being alone
In the night.
And to wake up with
Company in the room
In the morning.
And because she needs
Someone to mother.

A man needs a woman
To face himself.
But a man has no room
For the girl
Who lives in all of us.
A man wants a Woman!

So, why is it
Men become small boys
When they are with us?

MY HOT HEART

My hot heart
Soars eagle skyward updrafts
Into the face of wild wind
Piping piercing notes
Challenging velvet altitude
Ascending vertical air
Heavy feathered
Mocking storms
Rising higher than the gates of
Hidden heaven.

Wings in fixed position
Glide beneath patterned constellations
Spinning rotations east to west
Singing shrill disruptions
On wing beats
Exulting
In open spaces
Flying into the Sun.

No surrender
When the Call of the Wild is proven
Wings climb challenging air
Collide against the storm of you
Daring a roost so high it may be
Heaven's making.

SWEETHEART

There is no pretending anymore.
I walk on air.
Your eyes give me altitude.
Daily business abrupt stops
Skids
Encountering this
Soaring
Flinging, flying, billowing,
Fluttering
Here in my heart place.
You are my
Sweet
Heart
Of tenuous possibilities
And delicate desires.
I live
I breathe
I work
In steady streams mesmerized
Memorizing oasis shapes
Of your dozen ways of laughing
Nudging me up
Over the crest
Of your hillside
Where I tumble down
Airborne in somersaults
Into your
Sweet
Heart.

FLAWLESS

Your eyes
The color of autumn fields
Articulate sentences.
I want to undress.
Your smile stutters my inhale
I am conjugating verbs
Standing near me
I am covered in heat

Feral guitar strings hum
Long low moans music
Reaching for your hand
I shade my eyes
From revealing too much.
I have no skill
No cleverness
Except staring at you
Hoping you will laugh again.

Your track laid down for walking
Is a skyway to a million stars
The pull of gravity orchestrates
Singing a cry of you
In the back of my throat
I growl your name
Breaking out in gasps
Between my teeth
Your breath whispers in my mouth
I exhale skin into your sweat.
A kiss multiplies across my cheek
Winging into the curve of you.

Sinking soft through atmospheres
Meteor shower blazing
Striking earth
Hard
In smoking scattered scraps
Your starched shirt scratches me silk

Here\ Oh Look\
I lick my lips smiling into morning.

LULLABYE

I would make a song for you
Weaving willow words
Into fancy fabric
Embroidering a life
Of seasons turning
Around the sun.
Sky and green grass growing.
Meadows of wind blowing
Forest rains of gossamer mist
On mountains fertile with summer.
I would sing for you.
Bright bird wings shining
Purple flowers nodding
As clouds tumble
Turning somersaults
Falling out of the sky
Misting my cheekbones.

I would make a song for you
I would make a love for you
Round as earth
Easy as breath.
Warm as my grandmother's quilt.
Please?

BETWEEN SNOWFLAKES

Winter let down her hair this year.
I am tilting today in windward skies
Looking at you between snowflakes.
I miss you in winter.
Itching for you
This wet wool sweater
Turning skin rashy red bumpy.
My hunger needs scratched.
I confess
I am warding off spring
Wearing turtlenecks and wool scarves
Vests and coats and socks and boots.
You are so much more to me in winter.
Hold me lightly
I wait for that laugh that makes my
Hair tumble down.

CLAIMING LIGHT

We walked beaches
Scattered agates glittering wet
You played stories.
Picking cords
Strumming harmonies
Chorusing against unheard singing.
Out of the invisible in you
I realize visible edits.
Out of your spark
I claim light.
Out of your heaviness
I earn hardship.
Dream seeds
Told our fortune in rhyming syllables.
Beyond the tideline
We walked on water.
Time fell rusty oily in light
Recovered from comet tails of fire
By this ocean of oceans
I cannot enumerate
Nor repeat
Nor measure
Nor count
Nor cast.
I held your hand
Touching
Beyond sketched silhouettes.

PURELY SELFISH

This remarkable shining pining
Locked in moon-bright cadence
Heart beating everlasting wild
Unshared
Always mine
Is a purely selfish
Absolutely terrific
Scrumptious consideration
An ambitious collection
Engaged with tasty morsels
Dripping honey into my
Completely unkissed mouth.

This pure sentiment
Keeps me honest warm
On shivering nights rolled
Baby bowed
Sleeping fierce dreams
When frost creeps in my
Sleeping bag.

SUMMER THUNDERSTORMS

Waiting again
Through summer thunderstorms
Rolling heat lightning across mountains
Feeling dusk coming on
Long nights in backyard stillness
Chirping insects talk in the dark.

Waiting again
In downpours of silence
Absent conversations
Hover in monologues
Performed beneath night skies
Are you looking
At the same thundered sky
Missing me in sweet rain smells?

I gather cosmic dust
Surrounding halos of invisible material
From the endless creations of God
Putting old stars in straw baskets
Bringing the intersections
Of my harvest home
Brightening months yet to arrive
Spun on blurred edges.

HESITATIONS

We slide into each other
After summer finally sets us free.
This red bluffed river valley holds
Worn trails trudging toward outposts
Where lazy gold drenched mountains
Hold absence.

Here we are
Bare feet swinging
Kicking stones
In small creeks
Whistling
We connect oracles
From gods who deem us
Possibly not remarkable at all.

Here we are
Heads bent together
Guessing prospects
Arms entwined
Faces touching
Asking probing questions.

Here we are
Chattering children at recess
You lean into me
Shadowing my face
With kisses.

Here we are
Saying what need not be told
In the loop of conversations
Speaking careful queries
Reflected in each other's eyes
Pursuing answers.

Can you hear me calling
In long languid ballads
Lovers sing
In the back of their throats
In the tunnel of faraway autumns?
Do you see this beckoning woman
In your probing eyes
Asking a foretelling of futures
Prophecies of certainty
Revelations
Visions
A sign from Delphi.

We search meanings in
Polished window reflections
Looking over shoulders
In some downtown window
On the street side of life.

Look.
We are present tense beings
Overthinking irregularities
Stirring chaos in accumulated mud puddles.
We are a future hypothesis
Holograms twist images on sheer scarves
Folding three dimensional surprises
Wearing intercepted rainbow colors.

We are imprecise pastel sketches.
We are undeveloped film.
We are Norman Rockwell illustrations
Passing in a hurry
Writing a book
Hoping we have enough paper and ink.
Hoping we can find a publisher.
Hoping we can afford the printer.

In this tree veiled valley
Slow streams tickle enthusiasms
Soothing old rocks cradlesong wet
We shrine our moments
In common phrases
Wishing for extraordinary language.

You mystified
In close cut silence
Kiss me
Again and again
On the forest floor
Where all our youth is spilled
In dappled aspen light
Autumn colors dancing yellow festivals.

WHITE WASHED

Unlatched cell door
Locked tight
Swings wide
Erupting exposed
I run to your arms
Headlong
Rushing
Exploding into your
Untamed wilderness
Opening frontiers.

After so long quiet repose
In vaulted shadows
Belonging to yearning nights
Air surges riding sweet updrafts
Cool and clean
Emptying long chambered considerations
Dusty expectations
Stalled pauses waiting
For something to happen
Pushing stillness hurrying aside
Opening uncertain borders.

Allow bright light this
Clean whitewash
Fleeing winter's sobered rooms
Melting into spring waters
Runoff releases
Mountain fuel
Driving vast dangerous soul rivers
Leaping wet downward
Draining damp philosophies of others.

Blissful hello again
New day celebrates
It's Over\
Bursting sunbeams gather patterns
On green emerging buds
You are at last
Home.

OUR SONG FOR DANCING

Our song is an embrace.
My head on your chest
Taking in the smell of you
The touch of your bones
Under my fingertips
Thefeelofyourback
Strong
In our dance
In our song
Arms around my waist
Pull me close.

This moment is music
We make together
Eyes closed
Content
We found each other
In drumming beats of syncopation
Dancing
Together
Eyes closed
Swaying
Nearly standing still
Your breath on my neck
Perfection.
We found Our Someone
We can close our eyes now
Close our eyes to the world

Swaying
Inhaling
Exhaling
Breathing with resonant humming
Perfumed movements survive
Twice as long when
Embraces hum.

Our dancing song
Shuts windows tight
Pulls shades down
Locks doors
Clears the room.

We found our
Someone to hold
We found Our Person.
Even if it only lasts a minute or a day
This is how I think of Love
When I think of
Love.

EVERY GODDESS NEEDS

Every Goddess needs a strong man
Shielding Her from Dragons
And other plundering marauders
Who would maul and maim Her.

Every Goddess needs
A brave man
Who battles for Her
Protecting Her in the wilderness.

Every Goddess needs
A sturdy man
Standing behind Her
Covering Her back
When she pays attention to other needs
Baking bread
Clean-up jobs
Giving birth
Singing babies lullabies
Mending the wounds of others
Ignoring her own.

Every Goddess needs
A trustworthy man reliably guarding
As she sleeps imagining
Loving yet to come.

Every Goddess needs
A peaceful man
Folding Her in his arms calm
When She is wounded and grieving.

Every Goddess needs
A tranquil man reminding her
She is still beautiful.
When wrinkles deepen
Around the crinkles of Her eyes
And Her hair silvers
And Her hips grow round
And Her belly softens.

Every Goddess needs
An undisturbed giving man.
Harsh men need not apply.

HONEYMOON

Do you remember?
When you were
James Bond
In a rented, black tuxedo
And I was
Doris Day
In a white crepe gown?
We entertained
In Sausalito
Pouring wine down
Drunk on sex
Giggling at all
The street-side strummers
Sitting on the bay curbs
Singing fantasies.
We watched
Grey gulls climb blue sky
Lazy thermals
Riding high over Alcatraz.
Our own gliding illusions
Outsoared
Colored kites
Beneath the Golden Gate.

We stained all
The rumpled
Crumpled
Motel sheets
Between Red Bluff
California
And Winnemucca
With torrid excursions.
We were pure soulmates.

We talked
With perfect understandings
Reading from our script
Taking cues
Quite properly
Waving
At all the passersby.
Smiling.
Knowing.
No one ever loved
With our sophistication.

Trying on Sanskrit
We tripped along with
Peter Fonda riding easy
In our kalaidescoping
Reel-to-Real.
We explored
All of each other
Most of San Francisco
Dancing our hearts
On beaches
Of fine, fine sand.

We thought:
This is the most delightful
Movie
We ever starred in\

THE SLEEP OF SMALL HOURS

In the sleep of
Small hours
Your hand explores my outline
Nudging me hurriedly awake
Reaching urgent.
Aching stretching toward
Contact
My hips handles
My arms long songs
My hands squeaks and squeals
Greedy
Pulling me close
Pouring your body over mine
Kicking off covers
Spinning together
One lean yielding muscle
Pressing
Pushing
Seeking
Souls open
Wider than the sky can see
Tangled
In molten conversation
Sleepy urgent.
I am nearly asleep again
In the after-warmth of
Man/Woman conversations
Your leg
Sprawls carelessly
Over my thigh.
Wide-eyed I am struck
Amazed.
My mother was afraid
A man might do this with me.

MORNING

One night you asked
In the darkness
Of loving
As I reached out touching you
Moving close against
The consolation of your body
Seeking warmth
Why I love you.
I said "because."

We slept.
Two bears fitting together
Cozy tight in safe dens
Until white sunlight
Crept between cracks
In linen curtains
Framing blue walls.

Sleepy awake stretching
I found your eyes searching mine
The question
Gone
Only your grin
Warming my morning.

SLOW EXHALES

I am hot with your touch
Torched from your hands
Ink-stained fingers
Tracing outlines
Finding edges
Of my frame
Tasting the size of me
Sanding my textures
Smoothing my brow
Your mouth liquid honey
Searching
Valleys, ridges, curves
Finding wishes.
My skin alive
With your smell
All blushing drowsiness
I roll in your sheets
Round and safe and pink.
Firmness of your rib cage
Presses against my heart
Hands find
The flatness of your stomach.
Resting in slow exhales
I am heavy with wrapping
Against you
A package of silken occurrences
Silken skin
Silken radiation
Silken breath slow
Loving you all over
Again.
Soft sighs arrive cooling
Dreams begin pattering footsteps
Tiptoeing connections in rhythms of your sleep.

GREEN PILLOWS

Idling in darkness
Meditations silver dew dripping
Slowly sliding
Glistening cool
Along strands of
Sun-spun spider webs.

Coveting you.
Aching again
For your eyes
Hands
Breath
Smile
Kiss
Telling me
I Am.

If I could pillow myself
Beside your bright head
Watching your eyebrows rise
In surprise
I would not be so aware
Of your stillness
On the other side
Of this marriage bed
Awake with considerations
Twisting shadows
Across the ceiling
As madly as mine.

Come to me.
Let me rock you to sleep
On the cradle of my hips.

FOG

How utterly luscious
Lazy
Hazy
Cloudy
Thinking about you
Fogging all my senses.

I am vague
These days
I know.
You don't have to tell me so.

I am who?
I am where?
I am wandering
In and out
And round about
Exploring the Me of Me
The You of You
Thinking
Wouldn't it be wonderful
Being
Completely
Absolutely
Always
Impeccably
Predictable
Knowing something of
What is next?

But then
I'd lose my charm
Wouldn't I?

WALKING UNDER TREES

If I could tell you anything
          Which I can't,
                    Which I can't
                              Which I can't
Anything at all
Quietly
Safely
Softly
Mercifully
I would tell you my fear.

My fear
That sometimes prostrates me
Between cracks in the sidewalk
When I am walking home
Under trees
My fear
That I am unable to touch
Who I am
My fear that I wear
          Like a bead
                    Like a bead
                              Like a bead
However wrong or right.

If I could tell you anything
          Which I can't
                    Which I can't
                              Which I can't
Anything at all
          Quietly

                    Safely

                              Softly
                                        Mercifully

I would tell you my joy
That sometimes prostrates me
Between cracks in the sidewalk
When I am walking home
Under trees
At night
Fed by the music of God.

I would tell you
Of the lifting lilt of wonder
When I settle sleeping
With your hand resting on
The round curve of my belly
Your breath warm, globed
Against my ear.
Oh\
Then
How I dance with God
If I could tell you anything
        Which I can't
                Which I can't
                        Which I can't
Anything at all

        Quietly
                Safely
                        Softly
                                Mercifully

I would tell you this.

THE SOUND OF ART

If I could write my heart
In words
Carving a monumental permanence
You might begin
At the beginning of beginnings
Playing all the musical notes
Of this sonata
Musical score
Composition
Symphony
Me.

Language is an artful violin
Dragging bow rich round notes
Over strings of conversations
Contrasting tempos
Private orchestrations
Adagio
Allegro
Largo
Crescendo
Ritardando
Communicating compositions
Praising the art of sound
Our harmonies sleek.

Synchronization is required when
Composing any worthy opus.

Now my voice is dry dusty
Croaking hoarse
Broken soundboard echoes
Weary with overplaying
Spilling my abundance
Of words
Into damp silence.
Conducting a duet of futility.
Rewriting I chisel a fabled shrine
Honoring muteness.

Words after all
Are merely ordinary canisters
Storing moments.
You are after all more
Than any words can tune.
After all I am more
Than words can journey.
Let us give up making
Recorded histories together.

Yield the restless violin sighing
Hard ancient myths
Yearning music suppressed
There are no more words
To play violins and harps.

Great eternal stars collect
All the broken-hearted strings snapping
Extinguished sounds across
Timeless space spinning limitless
Voiceless recordings
Where we remain
Unspoken
Traveling speaking silences
Concealed.

BALANCING THE SOUL

In flashes of tomorrows
The world stops startled still
Galaxies release swirling light trails
Keeping orbits moving in alignment
Unaffected by my paralysis.

My children
You are like you never were
Spreading open before my eyes
Filling my evening with
Hundreds of Billions of stars
Celestial time rises with day break
Remains forever
Moving eternal
A solid pace of resilience.

I am beyond the power
Of language
Tangible pursuits meaningless
Living in private hallways
Hiding from repentance
Opening my worn collection
Of rasping personal history to you
You are Light
You are mine
Forever.

I am looking glass bright
A balancing act wobbling humility
Burrowing my face
In the scent of your hair
Looking at perfect you
My first prayers.

LISTENING IS A VERB

Pay attention please.
I have something important to say
Your eyes sky wander
Seeking cloudbanks of sunset
Where old wishes speak
Befores.

Pay attention please.
I have something important to say
If you turn and look
At our round earth
I am standing here
Present
Not past tense.

Pay attention please.
I have something important to say
I am weary of using myself
In absurdities and good-byes
I don't understand
In the first place.

Pay attention please.
I have something important to say
Before you put the fire out.
I love you.

Please.
Just this once
Turn around
Hear my heart speak
Because love you know
Doesn't happen very often

You and I are luckier
Than you know.
I've waited a thousand years to
Speak outloud
Without the usual lockups.
We only have ourselves to be afraid of
In the dark.

At the end of days
Conquest thrives
Undermines reaching
Pretends perfected peaceful peace
Falsifies an absence of cruel war
Restful relief a mirage
A random fixed point
Unidentified on a lost star map.

So leave the fire burning
On the river edge
Where futures disappear in undertow.
Let our flames be a beacon to old losses.
Later you might remember
I had something important to say
Just this once.

CRACKS IN THE SIDEWALK

The clock is ticking vengeance
The house is growling.
Please! come over.
Surprise me
Where I smile
Come to my bed
Surprise me.
Please! It's late.
I am becoming ancient
Second hands
Counting
Wasted time.
My hands ache to heat
Your skin.
Let my hair fall down.
Say the words!
Oh! Say the words!
Out Loud!
Please! It's late.
The house is growling.
Please! come over.
Take me further
Take me deeper
Take me where my heart
Rushes forward
Out of breath
And I have swallowed you
Backward
In traveling conversations.
Please!
Come over!
Touch me
Where I smile.

FLYING OVER WHITECAPS

Where are you traveling
These sultry salty days?
Storm winds swell skies

Unspilled rains fall.
We all yearn moments
Unfurling purple sails
Cutting crisp westerlies
Winging, expanding, extending
Trade winds filling canvas
Snapping
Running silk thrills throbbing
Howling windy loud outbursts
Piloting whitecaps
Seafaring far horizons
Sextant suggesting
Imaginations
Batten down the hatches.
If I could
I would set you free.
Climb your mast
Fly your distress flag
Morse Code an SOS
Send up a flare
Holler Mayday.
Half the declarations
Were your choice
While half of mine wait
For you to dock your boat.
Leave indignations behind
Watch the sunrise
Startle me with respect.
After all this time
I would do almost
Anything for you.
Almost.
Don't ask me to pack
Your suitcase.
I have decided to be dangerous.

TO BE CONTINUED

I said:
You don't say I love you anymore.
You said:
I washed the car today.

I said:
You don't say I love you anymore.
You said:
Did you get paid yet?

I said:
You don't say I love you anymore.
You said:
I'm here aren't I?

I said:
You don't say I love you anymore.
You said:
I am not really comfortable
Saying those kinds of things
Talking is your job.

I said:

Nothing.

NEEDING A LAUGH

Holding hands under overcast skies
Watching contagious raucous
Whitewater assaults
Agitating rocky outcroppings
Spurring boulders to repentance
We researched river memories
Smiling.

Too many new moons
Grew choked vines
Thorny hedges cactus bordered
Since the times we laughed.
I very nearly forgot
How your mouth crinkles
Before you collapse in grins
Telling stories
Recalling
How you throw your head back
When you are pleased.

Wind chapped river washed legs.
You dried my feet
Pulling socks over red toes
Laughing in growls.
We were an event of surprises
Holding us tight in
Before.

HARD THOUGHTS

Early morning hours
Are the hardest to pacify
Wanting to reach out
Touching familiarity
Instead of lying wide-eyed
Shuddering
Fluttering
Stuttering
Keeping corners company.

There never was
Satisfaction
Searching out cobwebs
On white ceilings
Tracing your patterns
Over and Over
Again and Again
Aware you are elsewhere
Over and Over
Circling hot air
With summer thirsts
Including how to kiss you.
Including how to kill you.

My appetites are empty
Of touching your smile
My favorite
Part and parcel of
Staring at you
When you are sleeping
My eyes on your face.

Perched on the sink chatting
Prattling back and forth
Speaking the language of futures
Silly crazy sparkling nonsense
Teasing playful full of ourselves
Watching you shave
Grinning juicy thoughts.

Early morning hours hesitate empty
Detention has no shade
Groping along summertime days
Gaps in dialog extend sighs
Defiant.
I am needing to be part of you again.

PERFECT LOSS

Who are you?
I journeyed far
Places
To touch you
This way.
Who are you?
I traveled speaking
Silence
For a touch
Like this.
What is this great burlesque?
This urgency of driving
Night highways in snowstorms
Into your arms
Just as you turn your back.
How can I let go of you
When I am rehabilitated of everything
Except violent celestial storms.

RITUAL BY ROTE

Tell me a God, Mama.
I need loving.
Tell me a life, Mama.
I need a friend
For later.
Tell me a hurt, Mama.
I don't think I can
Get up again.
Tell me a love, Mama.
So I can laugh
At the fool who keeps believing.
Tell me a God, Mama.
I need to pray
And I can't find anyone to listen.

VIGNETTE IV

Love fulfilled

Does not write poetry.

It is complete enough

Without adding

Aching words

of

Explanation

III Pruning

I thought that this the love I gave would always get me by

I thought that deep down lovin' was a hard time alibi

The Guitar Player

III Pruning

VIGNETTE V

The candle flame will last

Until the wick becomes an ash

What then of love

When fuel is gone

How flames the candle back?

No wax!

EITHER/OR

Either:

We lived together
Long enough
Words lost their
Function
Tying etiquette together
Memorized

Or

We don't need them
Anymore
Except conversations about
The kids
The dog
The bank statement.

Or

We lived together
Long enough
There are
No words.

ALMOST

Once.
We walked the tempo of valleys
Kicking fallen leaf smells
Into piles of crisp memorials
Talking bright feelings
Amused
As no one had ever spoken
Before.

Once.
We moved in drifted winter forests
Spotted in sunlight
Dappled with shadows
Under trees groaning harmonies
Layered with the weight of snow
Falling into jacket collars.

Once.
Hands touched skin.
Shaded eyes squinted
Casual observations.
Smiles rhymed philosophy.
Every sequence of sentences
Spoken undaunted.

Once.
Worried breath vigilant
Measured each absence
When skin on skin revived
Conversations on conversations
Layered with action syllables
Begetting words
Hearts on hearts
Painting a beautiful tree.

Once.
Time, that old thief,
Pretended to be on our side
Impatient with playing catch-up
In the full sleeves of ourselves.
We almost made it.
Excuses were bondage.

Then

We ran out of words.
Bodies carried on
Conversations of habit.
Motionless gods kept unblinking vigil
Followed our stuttering glazed
Discontinued closed eye breaths
Disrespect built
Stone walls cloistering wails.
Corners of summer purged us
The heat season gone.

Too many spaces
Too many absences
Too many sequestered minutes
Too many jump starts
Too much greed
Too much isolation
Too many shortage months
Between the ebb and flow
Of rivers drought dying
Streaming downhill yearning
Ocean frontiers.

But the calm port.
Oh\
The calm port you were\\

BLACK ROSES

Am I over you
Are you over me
Was I ever
Were you ever
Were we forever
Or were we never
A small illusion
Suffered a brief intrusion
Completely lost
Have we paid the cost
I am nothing anymore
Without knowing where you are
That somewhere in the night
You dream the candle of my light

A DAINTY DISH

I yield the field
Like so many long stems of
Buffalo grass
Prairie bending in icy blizzards
Looking sideways
Over my shoulder
Signaling war wounds.

I want to be touched easy
Without my unappreciated soul music
Needle scratched
Harsh counseled
Word bruised
Knocked down
Frayed artillery word exchanges
Explode my songs
I am no gossamer drapery
Hanging on hooks
Shredded in tatters
Torn ragged heckled bribed by
Crushing conversations
Requiring a crash helmet.

Isn't this a dainty dish?
Distressed four and twenty blackbirds
Baked in a pie
Forgetting how to sing?
Meanwhile.
The maid is in the counting house
Counting out confusions
Tallying collateral damages
Like winnings
In a poker game.

ALL OUR DREAMS

We are rupturing apart.
All our dreams
Popping
Balloons at the end
Of a carnival day.

We are rupturing apart.
In a rush of sad words
We shouldn't have
Spoken.

We are rupturing apart.
Spreading thick quilts
Of guilt
Covering us
Buttering burdens
For future reference.

We are rupturing apart.
Taking inventories
Of petty little
Didn't dos
Book keeping itemized lists
Accounting wrongs and woes
Intended for future
Evening prayers
When all we have is
Popped dreams
       Thick guilts
         And inventories of doubts
           Keeping us warm.

THE FIXED BLADE

I have gone on living with your fixed blade
Splitting the bone in my heart.
First love.
First loss.
First hope.
First dreams.
First ashes in a dying fire.
I have gone on living
The blaze of your skin
Melting me down
Becoming
One single moment of breath coming out fast
Voices shaking up stories
In an orchard of sleeping with you
Imagining
Growing blossomed fruit trees
While grass grows on ditches
Between rows
Sitting on branches singing
Waiting for a kiss
Between heart beats
Between sweet young saplings
Between early morning scents.

I have gone on living with your
Sharp broadhead
Severing lungs and heart strings
Watching fantasies of young trees growing
Gnarled memories
Groaning in wounded wooden skins.
Now our orchard mutters old
Timeworn strains of longing to bear fruit.
Ashy autumn fruitless trees
Scrape against each other
Groaning winter is coming.

Time cartwheels toward coffins
Whispering tall tales voiceless
Locoweed questions hang on for dear life
Surviving indecisions
Curving me war invaded
An archer's bow shooting
Fletched arrows
Drops me on my knees
Winter is coming.

You were my first seedling.
My first sapling.
My first prayer.
My first pruning.
My first of all dreamings.
The fletching still holds
Your bright bladed arrow
Remarkable
In the bone of my heart.

Trembling Tibetan prayer flags
Stutter mantras chanting
In my Rocky Mountain creases
Grass grows weeds
On barefoot ditches
Between orchard rows
Old trees croon cradlesong celebrations
Waiting for the chainsaw.

NEWPORT SUMMER

I spent a summer once
Roaming salt sand beaches
Under Newport's arched bridge
Cold Oregon tides running high past
The jetty where sea lions play with
Silver salmon.
I spent a summer once
Declaring liberties
Dancing visions on cliffs
Wading pounding surf
Writing long long longer
Stretched poetry
Stuffing words confused with
Philosophical self-hypnosis
In the hypothermia of supplication
Talking to myself
Muttering like an old woman
Shrinking at shore pine sharp needles
Surf claiming undisciplined high tides
Embarrassed.

I lost ballast in frigid seas
Heaving with forgetful numbness
My life boat leaking overloads
Straining
Threatening capsize
Searching fragmented
Sea polished shell shard
Thinking I was a potter
Instead of a digger in ruins
Dwelling in history books.
I bailed futility.

Residual delusions stirred
Waking on stony shorelines
Rebukes from Agate Beach
Soaked dried dream-seeds in chilly tides
Swimming crested arches of
Bitter sea swells.
Seagulls airborne squawk
Shrill witness to slow sinking
Merciless superstitions.

Fictions were personal
Tight walled sand mixing water
Mortar kept crumbling
My patching wouldn't hold.
I wrote a ream of poetry
Dreaming lucid
Under lighthouse incandescent lenses
Scanning the Pacific's rise and fall
Dashing out words on wet paper
Along with my intelligence.

My pulse skipped
In thready races
When shrimp boats
Came churning mighty
Across the jetty bar
Men with strong backs
Long hair wind flying
Pulling greasy rope lines
Shouting grins.

I looked hard for you
Even though I doubted
You had ever been as far west
As Oregon coastlines
In any of several passing decades
Later my poetry
Was honest
So I burned it.
Now, I wish I hadn't.
The dream I burned to cinders
Was in those ashes.

AND HERE WE ARE

Rain pouring
Sea salt corroding
Sun on skin hustling
The bloom of age spots
Hikes on trails never taken
Wading streams unlaughed
Conversations waiting behind unopened doors
Thorns pricking thinning blood drops
Splashing wet red on white towels
Older
Wiser
Slower
Surviving
Chilly betrayals drenched
In the absence of truth
Conversations so keenly high pitched
Ribs break
Knees collapse
Breath stops
Fists tighten
Sobs make mud puddles
Face down
In the funeral aroma of sagebrush
When harsh grief arrives enslaving.

And here we are.
Smiles warm other eyes
Seasons slide slippery
Over rolling tsunamis
Waning moons plead
For the weight of light arriving
Out of 238,900 miles of
Darkness with no oxygen.

Children disembarked with considerable
Fanfare and welcome distinctions.
Grew.
Left home singing.

And here we are
Startled faces sliding the gravity sag
Mirrors reflecting nothing important in
Two hundred thousand years
Frowns came out of nowhere
There are dry eyed hollow days
Enclosed in a humming beehive of
Warp speed hastening Black Holes.
The fatigued conquered always yield.

And here we are
After all this time
Wading knee deep in whatevers
Trying to stay upright
Trying to cross a barrier reef
Patrolled by sharks
Trying to speak something
Crucial
Out loud
Bang.

SWIMMING AT SEA

Wild waters in the Bering sea
Are not advised.
Accidental drowning hazards
In narrow northern straits
Initiate emergencies.
Extreme polar temperatures
Restrict conversations.

In your personal Arctic Circle
Snow bricked igloo
You may as well
Mush sled dogs desperate
Across shifting ice floes
Cracking ripping racing
Ruthless restless waters
Waiting for your weight
Sinking heavy under.

Swimmers fast descending
Lose body heat
Beneath hypothermic ice
Drowning.

I am sinking fast frozen
In your freezer glares
Stranded
With polar bears eating
Marooned seals
On disturbed snow
Licking blood.

I can't stay warm with you.
Keeping my head
Above your Alaska
Sub-zero distressed seas
Is a lost cause.
Unskilled swimmers
In frigid temperatures
For long periods
Treading open water circles
Is not recommended.

Why do you believe
I am your
Coast Guard?

I am up for grabs now
Headed for solid ground
Knowing I will be tainted
With loss
For the rest of my life.

If I stay
One of us will no longer be
And I am so afraid
You see
I am so afraid
The swimmer will be me.

MENDING CLOTH

Stunning
Thundering
Arm waving ranting
Incoherent
Dramas smash
Priceless china words
Flay me bare boned bloody
Damage forbids my voice
Without getting shot.

There are moth holes in this
Dark weaving.
Trust withers
Shaped fetal
Swaddled in doubts
Weft edges fray
Fabric decays
Unresurrected.

Even when the cloth is
Mended
The tear still shows.

NO MAGIC FLIGHT DUST
(TINKERBELL DOESN'T LIVE HERE)

You are leaving?
I feel you slipping away
Dripping solid silvered liquid mercury
Between tightly clenched
Freeing fingers
Following private maps
Seeking some mysterious
Never-Never Land.

I have no magic flight dust
Hurled over already revving wings
Ready for take-off.
I have no magic flight dust
Sprinkled casually crossway
On mutations of map corners
Guiding a GPS to Peter's
Second Star to the Right
For a swift descent
Among dreamers shocked fields
I have no magic flight dust
Where you brake hard skidding
Against the grain of the moon
Longing for anything not boring.
I have more grit than flinging
Pixie dust.

I will not follow you
On unpaid flights of mysterious cravings
To be somewhere
In whatever place isn't here.
You meticulously unbind us
With irrational prattling
Like a woman's long hair
Forced loose in hurricane winds
Standing in disturbed wakes
Of your Going Going Gone.
Where is the shade you gave?

Words are bitter bundles sleeping in
Cardboard boxes locked and loaded
In ruthless inarticulate daylight
Waiting for the firing pin
To strike the primer
Snap.
Crack.
Smack.

Sorrow drunken stumbles
Grumbling against
The empty pump in my chest.
Every unfilled mouthful of words
Lumps in my choked throat.
I am cracked glass with a bullet hole
Slivered in razor shards
Standing tongue-tied.
This is no small portion
Of theft.

Placing a lipstick kiss curse
On your photograph as you flee
South
Desert cactus
Stealing days of my life
Shortened by dulled dye fading
Colors

Amazed\
Staring startled
Blank-brained
Silent-blind
Speechless-dumb
Fallen-crumpled
Comprehending disintegration
Marching across decades
Where I live
A constant refugee.

NO NAMES

Night drops the sky shivering
Snow drifts squeak crusty
Under rubber boots
Stepping carefully.

Storm flurries stagger
Winter walkers
Wolves prowl polar forests
Moonlight freezes
Blizzards blind.

Yellowed letters tucked in small packets
Faded ink spells past revelations
Folded paper
Blue ribbon gray-eyed
Frayed
Removed
Opened
Exposed oxidized
Smelling old
Moldering in broken drawers
A shabby bureau
Needing paint
Forgotten poetry
Crumpled corners tidy bundled hoarding
Chilled memories
Sentenced to extinguishing fire.

I wonder which of us is swallowed up?
I think I should remember
But we both know
People never do.

INTO THE WIND

We sail on different oceans
Of disappointment.
How can I give you
Latitude or longitude
Or advise on filling the pitch of your sail
In whirlwind gales
When my own ship is sinking
Out of sight?

Only calm winds smooth an ocean.

Who ever said there were
No conditions
On my generosities?
Whatever I did for you
I did for myself.

Only time can green a battlefield.

I won't negotiate who I am.
Who are you to say
I am not a
A sound investment?

SPIKED BOOTS

It hurts like hell.
But I'm
Making a getaway
This time.
I smell you
On the pillowcase
Even now
Heat rises from
Empty sheets on
Your side of the bed.
You haven't quite left yet
But scraps you leave
Make me cry.

Our bed is an
Uninhabited planet.

Who will I roll against
Nesting close
In the middle of the night
When I walk alone
On walls
With spiked boot debates?

It hurts like hell.
But I am breaking out
From all your brazen
Robberies
This time.

Your one little guitar song
Halts me paralyzed
Each spiked boot step
Leads to escape.

If I don't watch out
I'll be singing the same old
Out of key sheet music
Again
As if thinking about you
Doesn't bring me to a halt.

I'll be doing the
Same old conversations
Again
One small arrow thought
I am slain
On the ground
Again.

I have to stay vigilant
I have to stay alert
I have to sharpen
Spiked boots
I have to lock the door
Close the window
Turn lights off
Against your larceny
This time.

I AM BUILT FOR WALKING

Here it is again.
Truth in the bed
Hammering me.

I am not some skinny
Scrawny
Lanky
Thin
Snub nosed
Tiny
Size 6
Cutie pixie scrawny gaunt
No meat on the bones
Woman
With hips like a boy
Thighs no bigger around than
My calves
Collar bones sticking out
Far enough
To hang clothes on
Nor am I a long blond hair
Streaming over your pillow
Eyes blinking coyly upward
So you can sigh.

I am a vigorous woman
Built for walking
Hundreds of miles
Before breathing hard.
I am made to carry babies
On broad hip bones
Carry arms in war
Dragging the wounded home
Burying the dead
With my bare hands
If required.

I am armed to defend you
And ours
And mine.
I am equipped to survive famine
Drive a team of horses
Plow a field without whimpering.

I am built
To hold you
Tightly bound in the heated cradle
Of my hips
Wrapping sturdy thighs
Strong and relentless
Around your back
Pulling you so hard
Into my soul
You are lost in my earthquake.

I am no willowy wimpy
Simpering
Spoofed hair
Pierced eared hooped earrings
False chipped fingernails
Classic magazine big eyed waif
With a boys butt
In a magazine.

Here is blunt truth
In my bed
Hammering me
With your desire
For someone else.

GETTING IT OVER WITH

Hey!
Put the knife down!
Will ya!
You don't want a killing.
You want to hit something.
Hard.
You want
Revenge.

Hey!
Put the knife down!
Will ya!
You don't want death.
You lust
To hurt somebody bad
The way you hurt now.
After the way you hurt me.

Hey!
Put the knife down!
Will ya!
You don't want a killing.
You want a bit of blood spatter
Making your point.

So I will turn my cheek
Into your fist
If it will make you
Go.

Later, we can cry
Alone
And wonder
Why?

THE RUBBLE WOMAN

In the middle of this rubble
Remains of falling apart
I cannot explain
Or even understand
I sit down worn thin
The Rubble Woman
In the shattered trash
Of bombing runs
Remembering
First time war.

Our words were
A roar of rapids
We rode
In white-water fever
We couldn't say it all
Fast enough
Then.

Featured dialogs tumbled
Sprayed happy hopeful against
Swirling currents of anticipation
Churned us round and round
In whirlpools
Into each other's arms
Each other's words
Discovering lines in poetry.

Our cascading fiction
Urged us on
Digging paddles deep
Advancing swift undercurrents
Composing the next narration
Determining limits of endurance

Let's see what surprises
Meet us
After we catch our breath
At the intersections of
Sharp edges.

When did our river
Flood beyond boundaries
Slow down
Roll wallowing
Cornered in frog water
Spinning murky undertows
Found under cooling shade
Along canal bank willows
Wordless?

JUST THIS ONCE

Just this once
Do you think
A little more empathy
Could fasten on the
Tiniest moment
Of indulgence
With my leniency needs?

Just this once
Could we refuse
Judgment hardening our lives
And make a fist
Against distractions.

Just this once
Do you think
We could be kids
At a carnival afternoon?

I am not a combat zone!
Taking away my words
Conducting siege on speech
Encounters die a hard death
Cracking bone marrow
Infects wounds.

You are a combatant
Flailing blindly
Shouting insignificance
Practicing mayhem.

I am your sacrifice
And you don't know it yet.

RE-ARRANGE-MEANT

Reading, reading, reading
Alone, alone, alone
Crazy
Writing rearrangements
Dreading
Slow dances of madness.
The lunatic fringe
Appears peeping
Through troubled windows.

Misplaced, misplaced, misplaced
And you?
A short walk away
A phone conversation away
A breath
An energy
Away.

Reading, reading, reading
Throwing books
Violent
Hurting walls
Ripping out pages
Eating them raw
The lunatic fringe
Appears below in streetlights
Face down in grass.

Struggling ten-thousand times
Failing again and again
Comprehension denied
Expressionless collateral damage
As if you are a holy mission
Imposing the challenge of saints
For the ten-thousandth time today.

The lunatic fringe repositions
Vocalizing solos
In this crazy room
Rearranging waltzes.

The lunatic fringe
Appears in yellowed wallpaper
Heckling, jeering, taunting
Injured walls
Broken book stacks
Spider web crevices
Cracked reflection in mirrors
Reveals a woman rearranging
Smoothing pillowcases
Counting silverware.
The lunatic fringe
Answers trembling
Knowing you lay in bed
Arms around another
Concentrations on another
Laughter pouring over another
Mouth on another
With your skin fantasies
Entertained by another.
I have stopped wanting donations.
I have stopped wanting adoptions.

Relocation is work best handled
Late at night
Peeling yellow wallpaper
From crumbling sheet rocked walls
Digging ditches in drywall
With fingernails daily harvesting
Daily rearranging
When the money-changer cheats.
Outside the lunatic fringe shudders
Caressing ears of yapping wolves
At the door.

I COULD· NO· I WON'T·

I would like to find
Some kind of inward courage
That stick-to-the-ribs bravery
Like the oatmeal
Mother placed steaming
On the breakfast table.

I would like to find
That awful thought
Motivating pride
To act.
A projection of character
Driving my pointed pen
Giving it impetus
To write
One Long Last Good-bye!
Or stab you in the throat
With an icepick.
Now, there's a thought.

I am sucked hollow eyed
With this passive yielding
Skin flinching with contusions
Pouring my full pitcher
Of attempted devotions over your
Uncertainties
Baying like dogs hunting the fox.

I would write
GOOD-BYE
In capital letters
With fingers of blood
On walls.
A message even you could
Understand
All the while wanting
To watch my pen scratch
HELLO again.
Besides
I want my Good-Bye
To hurt you violently.
I don't write it now
Because it won't.

SCRIBED SAND

Yesterday
Beaches broken sand invited
Stories
When wind blew bitter
I dug down deep
Carving
Ancient names
Scribing tiny droplet clouds
Old hungers condensing
Soaked with befores
Salt water wet with
Cancellations
Engraving revoked names
Together side by side
My crouching shadow
Hunched coiled upside down.

Temperatures too low for
Human thawing sentiments
Digging sand stick in hand
Writing
Tide foam extending
Grey bubbles flooding
Neglected empty beaches
Speculating
What the fuss is all about.

Considering
Our long voyaging
Separate years
Tasting salt air
Salt tears
Salting me shriveled
Preserving me.

Turning around
I became Lot's wife.
Drawing hearts
Yours traveling
Mine beautifully unclaimed
Calligraphy in sand
Describing
Scribing
Executing
Sending a message
Dot dashing across space
Toward the rim of the sun
Heating descent.

I stepped aside
Tender
Sat back staring
Electric possibilities
Names sometimes
Encompass
Or is it embrace?
Tides divide words.
First letters blur
Run away in rivulets
Stream down beach gullies
Sea claimed washed
Sea salt or salt tears?
A covenant of salt.
Lot's wife
Blinking
Names
Captured Sons and Daughter
Claimed
Reaching.

UNMAILED LETTER

I wonder where you are now.
Somewhere in that brown prickly
Sharp shaped southwest desert
You are growing muscle on bones
In your brand new life.
In the middle of your new life
In the middle of your middle aged new life
And my middle aged surprise
I wonder if you will ever
Read this
Thinking hard.

I perpetually feel you in doorways
Under the stairs of my life
I run in fast forward film clips
Toward you.
Remembering with eyes wide closed
Running
Tripping
Falling down
Repeatedly.
Other voices whisper harsh repetitions
I am not enough.
When I am old and very thin
Clutching fingers twisting
Sweaty sheets
Body melting
Folding inward
Knotted fetal
Moving toward oblivion
Will I still be running with scissors?
Consecrating holy conversations
With votive candles?

When I am old and very thin
Will I babble nonsense phrases?
Worry tattered boundaries of lost words jabbering
The real thing
The real deal
The real drop-off of corked sentences.
Keen secrets hushed unspoken?

Stepping over ruined flesh
Collapsing into practiced footsteps
Out of breath
Will I move forward entering mirrors
Unceasingly crossing a room waiting to fall
Carrying all the colored threads I spun crooked
Calling out in an unironed voice
Pushing forward attempting trapped talking
Shining with astonished confessions and forgiveness.

Then as my children walk by
I'll stop.

VERTIGO

Flying over Albuquerque in twilight
I never fantasize well.
No erotic passion in the desert.
I dream I am crossing Rockies
Pushing pack animals
In frosty moonlight
Ready and waiting to homestead
On the edge of an aspen grove
Next to high ledges of mountains.

Even thinking about
Falling out of the sky
In this plummeting modern jet engine
Failure
Produces less dread than those old days
When casual betrayals
Included you
Included myself.

I wake up dying now
While children watch
Lying about this
Brand new broken heart
Uttering frozen cocktail smoothies
About mending stronger than before.

Dark clouds veil this hollow plane
Prayers descend night's laddered
Misplaced moonlight.
I come dropping down from
Oregon forests into
She-wolf dens
By way of slantways electric glow
In a rain of detritus

Skidding across this desert runway
Painted in bold faced fonts.
The airport screen announces arrivals
In small green hard to see letters
I've been away too long
I am passe.
I'm all out of love anymore
And nobody looks up.

WE WERE AFRAID

I should have wept.
I did.
Then I wore my armor.

I should have written obscenities
On all the walls
Smashed dishes
Broken chairs
Kicked the door in
Set the room on fire.

There were things I should have said
There were things I could have said
Veins I should have opened
Hoping to break your heart
Knowing it would just break mine.

Nothing helps a woman
Left behind when
A man makes excuses.
A man always wandering away
In the first place.
Every word ever spoken
A memorized recorded mantra
Borrowed from an answering machine.

This is the part of the story
Where it isn't
Enchanted Evening
Anymore.
This is the part of the story
Where we turn our backs
Break ranks
Defend the territory
Plant landmines
Grimacing.

This is the part of the story
We were afraid would happen.

YOUR SHARE

Our well of deep sorrows
I drank to drunkenness
A few friends
Who weren't too busy taking sides
Stayed around for the duration

Said:
Isn't she amazing!
Drinking so much
And still be
Sober.

They would not see
This reeling step of soul-loss
Slurred speech
Garbled grieving
Gutted anguish.

I hid war-wounds
That never should have been wounds
With shrugs and walk abouts.

Time has not stopped
Water seeping through brick wall
Compromised connections
Fill my water wheel with flooded failures
Language sinking in undertow.

I am full to sickness
Remembering how high notes soared
When the guitar strummed
Pulsing melodies beginning a chorus.
Thinking now I shall go mad

If your fingers
Do not brush my skin
And your mouth cover mine
One more time.
How do you live with
Your
      Share
           Of
              The
                  Well?

LAST DAYS

I don't put up much of a fight
Anymore
One embrace you can have me
I don't hurt
Too much
Nowadays
Although I'm not sure
I can get up again
Unless you help me
Mock the fool
Who keeps on believing.
I can't even tell you why
Because I need to pray
And can't find anyone home.

STONE BONES

Honeyed second hands drink
This taste in my mouth
Luscious
Juicy
Ripe
Succulent
Delicious
Salivating
Ageless wistfulness
When you launch your voice
At me across the stratosphere.

Even these old moss covered
Unkept stone bones of mine
Lying unexplored for eons
Along the banks of streams
Turning toward the sun
Can be surprised.

This ancient flood
In a disappearing skin canoe
Dawdles along now
Watering maudlin withered gardens
With a head full of photographs
Fading colors gathered
By the gods or goddesses
Occasionally passing by
Splintering these porcelain bones
Sizing me up for coffins.

I have trouble at borders.
My conversations are performed
On coastlines brave with rhetoric
The stones of Demosthenes arguing
In my mouth.
No paragraphs emerge.
None at all.

There are no sublime motivating phrases
Notched fragile in high tides
Dashed against stone pillars
Ragged debris of storm furies
Crooked with the weight of scars
Polished strong again in happy colors
Smoothing me beautiful
On beaches were I must have
Walked
With you
Once or twice
Before.

WISHFUL THINKING
A Quixotic Romp in Stylistic What-If-ness
OK, DAMNIT. IT'S A SHORT STORY

If, after all these long years
These spiked with dead dreams dying years
I could meet you for an afternoon
At the Hilton
I would probably spend a small fortune
On one new outfit
Purchased at Saks Fifth Avenue
Where I have never ever shopped.
It would be totally chic
Enormously expensive
Stunning enough to cover my self-conscious
Insecure
Chirping
Exposure of nerves.
Some swanky outfit you would approve of.
I would hire a consultant to help me.

If I could meet you for an afternoon
At the Hilton
I would diet for two months
Even though I don't need to lose a pound
Because I am one package of
Not petite self-doubt
Yielding to the timorous whims of
One can never be too thin
American women No Hips Allowed culture.
I admit I would starve
Until bones pierce my hip skin.

If I could meet you for an afternoon
At the Hilton
I would shave my legs twice\
Buy a new perfume
All my underwear would be brand new
Expensive
But none of that complicated
Alluring lace trimmed
In neon colors.
That's for hookers.

All the time I shop I would think
Why am I doing this?
I would use Bianca
Two spritzes of deodorant
Get a new haircut and a pedicure.
Biting my nails
I would avoid looking in mirrors.
Mirrors only remind me of time passing harshly
Like the blitzkrieg
Over my skin.

I would expect you looking Brooks Brothers crisp
Starched shirt classy wearing
Razor sharp creased slacks
Smelling English Leather familiar.
Better yet British Sterling
It probably still suits you.
The smell, your smell, that British Sterling smell
Always turns my head in a crowd
I become a scent hound questing.
By now you've probably switched to Grey Flannel.

If I could meet you for an afternoon
At the Hilton
I would never wait self-consciously in the lobby
The older image of a girl pacing
Before her first date.
No waiting in the lobby is not for me now.
I'd tip the maTtre 'de
Something I learned from you.
(Lord we were young.)
He would summon you to my table.
Seated feverishly worried you won't recognize me
I've grown so old and you, of course,
Are forever young to me.
Worse, I would not recognize you
Waving stupidly at that other handsome man
Wearing the perfect sport coat and fabulous tie.
I would end up stuffing my fingers in my mouth
Sighing in mortification, "OH\" Oh\ My\"
Wondering yet again what the hell I was doing here.

If I could meet you for an afternoon
At the Hilton
We would greet each other "Hello"
Laugh at being so damned self-conscious
Lean in for that small apropos kiss on the cheek
Saying, "You look just like I remembered."
"You haven't changed a bit."
Inside, we would be thinking
"Oh Lord, The Changes\"
(If you only knew. I've grown up. Sort of.)

If I could meet you for an afternoon
At the Hilton
You'd ask the waiter to bring the menu
We would chit-chat about weather

Your flight to the West Coast
My flight north
Airport conditions we encountered
In the middle of somewhere
We never thought we would be again.
We would talk about constant rain
Along the Pacific coast
How splendid fall colors are in the East
When Fall sweeps up over hills above rivers.
How we miss snow.
Were our families' fine?
What did we name our children?
Whoever thought we would be parents?

If I could meet you for an afternoon
At the Hilton
We would keep our eyes in touch with the salad
Stabbing tomatoes and cucumbers
With unspoken long conversations
Covering blank spaces with coughs
Gently picking our way along
Porcelain edges and silverware.

Then

We would look up at the same time
Eyes speaking the forever unspoken.
We would chuckle
Laughing at ourselves.
Only after that startled stare
Could we
Would we finally
Sit back and lighten up.

If I could meet you for an afternoon
At the Hilton
By the entree in the same cozy rhythm
Finishing each other's sentences
Our conversation advances.
We are at the "Do you remember?" stanza.
We would say, "yes," and "oh, yes\"
We would only talk of good times
Friends we loved
Silly jokes and being rescued.
We would skirt around discomfort
Like you pull peas away from slices of cold roast beef
At a banquet you found yourself surprised to attend.
We would be warming up.
Our dialogue smooth familiar
Sticking to our current lives.
Then one of us would say
"So, how are you, really?"

By then afternoon would fall narrowing the day
Elbowed by other commitments
Other loyalties
Belongings we owe
People we love.
Sun sliding down the sky
When we finally encounter
All the years passing and changing
Spinning and wandering
Weaving and twisting
Loving and unloving
Our steadfast words still marooned.

If I could meet you for an afternoon
At the Hilton
I would be sorry seeing the day flee.
We would say, "so long".
"Take care"
"Promise to keep in touch"
"So wonderful seeing you again."
Our hands would bump as we stood up
Folding the linen table cloth over
Uneaten plates of food hiding
Tenacious thoughts
Terminated conversations
Holding our vanquished breath.

For a dozen heartbeats we pause
Smiling one last time
Lean in suddenly holding on.
A soft kiss goodbye.
Something we could not do before.

Then

Looking at your watch
Heading out the door
Hailing your taxi
Looking left and right
Dashing up over the horizon into your life
No backward glance
Just forward urgency.
I turn away ever so slowly
Carried on tiptoeing feet
To the underground parking garage.

Sitting still
Oh\ so very, very motionless
In my rental car for a long, long, long
Naked tic toc tic toc time moving forward
Breathing
Breathing again
Exhaling ever so slowly
Stopped.
Night falls down around headlights.
Starting the engine
Taking deep breaths sounding gasps
Looking backward over my shoulder
I would wonder-- would we both be thinking
"Thank God that's over."

Or would we?

SAFEKEPT

Inside the old envelope
Saved on shiny photo paper
Forty-four years ago
Two faces appear
Black and white images
He and She
Together
White on white
Black on black
Snapshot stopped
A disrespected passing moment
Nesting disregarded
Sliding loose into fingers
Knobby aged.

Ohhhhhh.
There they are!
Decades reversed.
Time tipping over
Backwards in a chair
Spills knotted devotions restrained
Under lock and key
Ambushed today by a nondescript
Aged photo
Black and White.

Look!
Take a breath.
Step back.
Breathe.
Glimmering smiles
High spirited purpose
Standing side by side.
Aren't they wonderful
In this moment of not even
Looking ahead?

See that cocky self-belief?
He is enjoying her arm on his shoulder
And possibly the smell of her
Pleased in his suit and tie.
See that serene confidence
In her almost smile?
She leans graceful against him
Draped on his body
Possessive.
He grins huge.

Look at those two kids
On glossy paper enjoying themselves
In a captured net of stillness
Their connective tissue frozen
Forever unassailable
Permanently
Eternally
Floating in a crafted pose
Leaning black and white
Together in desires
Unaware of thirsty hungers
Or mistakes prowling in corners
Waiting for self-made sorrows.
Look\
There they are
Dressed in black and white smiles
Snap.
A photo from a camera requiring film
Sold in a garage sale
Somewhere unremembered along the way.

They are
Everlasting in black and white
As they once believed they
Must be.

Can you see fire embers
Sparking between them
Even though the print
Is black and white?

Odd now.
Knowing there was no growing old
Together.
All that glowing intensity
Shimmering in
Black and White honesty.
Look\
Just Look\
They are enjoying each other
Radiant Bright
Dazzling
In their black and white eyes.
Odd now
The absence of volumes.
Books, notebooks, diaries, journals
Photo albums, scrapbooks, love letters
Collections not completed.
Intensity emptied.

This long ago photo
Free falls from a forgotten envelope
Stuck in pages of an unread book
Delivering bitter sweet uppercuts
With a fatal knockout punch
Ripples in my heart.
Beauty and catastrophe together
Laughing
Before weeds
These naive kids forgot to pull
Grew beanstalks no one could ascend

Suddenly requiring a time machine
Hurry. Rush. Speed. Stub my toe.
Breathless.

Climb in that pose
That moment
Inhabit those two far away people
One more time.
Shout warnings
Grab lighted wands
Wave off a certain crash landing
Signal slow down not a safe configuration
Instead this sticky dry mouth
Spitless with melancholy homesickness
Parks heavy on my panting chest.

I need to put on a helmet
Run red lights
Tell people get out of my way
Honk my horn
Flash my lights
Put my foot down hard on the gas pedal
Radio communications ahead
Resume signaling
Shout stop! Damnit Stop!
Pulse pounding shocked
Out of breath
Delirious with peeking at
He and She
Together
Forty four years
Later.

Here in my palm sweating hand
This black and white photograph
Taken by a camera
Sold in a garage sale
Along with the guitar
And a jar of cinders
Unfolds sweet bitterness
Crosses miles
Years
Decades.

Nearly half a century
Reaching to grip
The noise of Nothing.
Leaping into recesses
Long ago locked away
Knocking me over frail
This cosmic photographic collision
Is a stun gun.

Once more
That stale smell of Promises
That word Forever
That sober Truth after a binge
Grasps me in twisting barbed wire
Enclosing the pasture of loss.

Two kids
Beautiful in discovery
Still learning
How to shine
In the possibilities of
The red love knot.

ORATIONS

I will be at your funeral
Standing in the back of the broad tent
Covering clipped green cemetery grass
Shading all those many, many, many
Who come from near and far paying respects.
They will salute you
Under the canvas asylum of dimness
Where chairs set in elbow close rows
Hide tears of missing you fiercely
Casting small rainbows of eye wet honor
Against bundled flowers.
Under the tent it will not matter
Whatever weather is manifest
On the day they bury you.

I will be the one wearing
A large broad-brimmed hat
Wrapped with a long black veil.
I will smile in unknown quiet
My lipstick red.
Your children will look up whispering
Who is that?
Who IS that? Who is that woman?
That woman in the long black veil
Who is she?"

I will smile mysteries
Tears leaking down shrunken cheeks.
The dilated sob I stifle wraps tight enigmas
Sheltering harmonies and riddles.
Your child will approach saying
Did you know him?
Did you know our Father?

I smile with vanishing thoughts
Saying yes\
Your child will say
How?
How did you know him? Our Father?

I lean in whispering
I knew him when he was a Singer of Songs.
I knew him when he was Mister Twelve String Guitar.
I knew him when his motorcycle
Made roads disappear.
He lived on the edge of wildness
Wearing a motorcycle jacket backwards
In an ice storm protecting someone
Clinging to his back.
His fingers froze that night.

I knew him when he was mountain music
His chorus of chords strumming love beats
Before the first sorrows brought tears heavy
Falling where mountains stand firm guard
Over eons of stunning dreams
Written in ancient words.
Your child will say
When?
When was that?

I will smile mysteriously
In my large broad-brimmed hat
With a long black veil and whisper
In the beginning long ago
When his singing named The Rockies home.
Child it was before your time
And he loved you absolutely."

OR

You will come to my Wake
Because I will die first from dreaming too much.
My ashes will be neatly composed in an urn.
It will be the first time I am ever composed.
The party will be noisy, raucous and cheeky
With only a few people attending.
They will shout out epic tales
Play old rock and roll as it used to be.
Celebrating.

The party will begin with a dedication by
Talking Heads shouting about
Burning Down the House.
There will be no odes to heroism or my ambitions.
My sons will toast me with beer
Telling hilarious heartfelt stories.
My daughter will crack jokes and dance.

You will be the man in the Armani suit
Arriving at the front door
Paying your respects.
Over boisterous disorder
My children will look up suddenly
Whispering with their fair haired heads together
Who is that?
Who IS that man?
Who is that man in the Armani suit?
My child will approach saying
Did you know her?
Did you know our Mother?
You clear your throat
Suddenly stuck from
Holding the shapes of riddles and sighs.

Leaning in you whisper
Yes, I knew your Mother.
My child will say
How? How did you know her?

You grin that heartbreaking grin saying
I knew her when her waterfall laughter
Cascaded fire over my heart
In a cold river.
My child will say
When?
When did you know her?
With silent tears inscrutable
Sliding uneasy down thin cheekbones
You smile mysteriously saying

I knew her in the long ago beginnings
When she danced untamed on edges
Of wordless wildness filling the sky with bliss.
She clung to my back on a motorcycle
During an ice storm
Laughing in my ear
Daring me to drive faster.

I knew her in the beginning
Before the first canyons of sorrow
Creased her smile.
Child, it was before your time
And she loved you absolutely."

POEM FOR TWO VOICES

1
Hello
Old Love
In the dying of my dreamings
You wait
To say
Hello again.
Wait
For my return
Back to you
With you
From you.
Across our separate years
Do you ever have a backward glance
Reaching for me again?
In this night dream
Here you are
Settled in shadow
All alone dreaming.
It is the only place
You live now.

2
In this fevered night-vision
My hand patting you
In the old familiar
Memorized repetitions
Our spaces warm sweetness
Out of breath
Out of soul.

1
Remember?
Beyond the need for night dreams
We played a child's game
Of tug-of-war
You and me
Yanking
Pulling
Pushing
Until the rope frayed
Came all unstrung
Hung in hemp shreds
Slack.
Then
We bequeathed each other
These night dreams.

2
Here you are fading again
Old love.
Sun bright morning blanches
These wisdom visions
Blurring you through
The pinholes of time
With sneak peeks at remains.

I am surprised again
Opening my eyes
Finding the room empty
Wobbling on bare feet
Inhaling a faint familiar fragrance
Savored on the tip of my tongue
A perfumed elegant melancholy
A memory essence of my becoming
All alone.

SAUSALITO REDUX

That Sausalito day!
I memorized every nuance
Music playing dockside
White cap blue sky wind ringing
Sitting on curbs
Wine on my tongue
The brush of fingertips
The sweat on your back
The quiet dark room asleep
I memorized that day
Not knowing how much
I would need it
Later.

PRAYER

Please, God.
In the middle of all this
Vain repetition
Going through the motions
Taking care of everybody else
Mumbling about salvation
Mourning the unspoken
Is it alright to squeeze
Something out of the orange
For me?
Please?

Once more before I die
Let there be a
First time
Again.

Please God.
I am needing
A new beginning
Or at the very least
Someone to kiss me properly.

VIGNETTE VI

I said,

I do not

Love you

Anymore.

I lied

To make you go

Sowe

Like

Pythons

Would cease

Swallowing

Each other

Whole.

Clear Cut

Way Over Yonder in the Minor Key

There ain't nobody that can sing like me

Woody Guthrie, Bill Braff

VIGNETTE VII

If you try to touch

This peering over my chasms

Thinking my mirror yours

You will hear hard

disappointments.

God forbid your grasp on me

I am for my own keeping.

EAST OF JESUS

Somewhere
East of Jesus
Is a dwelling place
Holding dark matter
A nebula of our internal universe
A super-nova paroxysm
Between joy and sorrow
Between love and unloving
Between birth and fear
Between Holy.

Somewhere
East of Jesus
The heavy pull of gravity
Projects our dualities
Attempting symbiosis
One with another.
One.
Another.
Striving.
Weaving a mesh of commonalities
With uneasiness
Aching
Separated
Etched grooves on brittle glass.
Wearing gloves
We carve ourselves in spiked inches
On slippery foreign landscapes
On the dark side of the moon
Where coyotes lament.

Somewhere
Between Dark and Light
Between weight and weightlessness
Looking for salvation I reside
Somewhere East of Jesus.

Somewhere
East of Jesus
Is the finish line
Where God finds
Redemption between our potholes.
The road is empty now
And I have far to travel without
A hand to hold.

THE FRAME OF SPEECH

After the long dark
I glow bright
Searching lake darkness
Mouthing memories outloud
Whispering unspoken futures
Sounding out syllables
Of tumbling stars orbiting.
I am the language of longing and regret
I am the alphabet of hope and smiles
I am the sound of letters being emptied on paper
I am the dialect of forfeiture and gain
I am the meaning of expansion and shrinkage
I message music.
Will you hear me?

My drifting thoughts
Dissolve distance
Escape in starships gliding
Eager daylight revelations
Where promises are finally kept
Speaking stillness
Alert
I have no motive
Except scriptured conversations.

Aurora Borealis sparks electrified.
Detonates light displays
Dazzling polar hemispheres
Envelops me in neon
Scents of long ago
Autumn ripeness
Escapes fallen leaves
Waiting for your return.

Carefully pardoned from my
Testing time
I am wrapped round and round
Packaged with ribbons
In the frame of speech
Hushed
Whispering hours fail sounds
Holding my stilled breath
Voiceless hostage.
"Shhhhh."

I walk awake
Under trees dressed in roses
Facing east
Where poetry
Surrenders
The last oblique truths.
Picking up my pen I begin again.

UNADORNED

You who later read me
Will never guess this dark crevasse
Of hesitations tripping boots
Over cliff extremes
Unadorned
Raw
In prairie fires
The cliff verge
Of my urge
Stops all momentum
Freezes hesitations
Prevents the sublime leap
Free falling twirling hesitations
Sustaining acrobatic somersaults
From slanted canyon rims
When the nervous herd
Stampedes toward the buffalo jump

CARRIED AWAY CAPTIVE

People leave.
Our disenchanted century
Has a name for it.
Personal Growth.
Growing Apart.
Nothing in common.
Social justice.
Finding myself.
PTSD.
Bookkeeping injuries.
Boredom.

Another list of extravagant
Soul dislocated
Self-serving mythologies
Media posted
Developed while gazing in the mirror.

People leave.
Love stumbles
Loyalty breaks
People choke
Fold inward to their knees
Shriveled by the absence of sound
With no voices singing hymns
When they are left
Too long
In a butterfly jar.

Did you not notice how hard it is
To open that rusted mason jar
With no holes poked in the lid?
Carbon dioxide corrodes
Stale empty air suffocates
The caterpillar dies.
You did not know that?

People leave
Don't come back.
But that doesn't mean
You don't need to ask us
To stay.
There are those of us
Who can't get home again.
We would like to try
But fear is dangerous slavery.

So leave the key under the mat
Turn on the porch light
Put a candle in the window
Hold out your hand
Send us a post card
Don't be afraid.
Tell us.
Tell us
You always waited
Dreaming we would
Turn around
And come Home.

COMES THE DAWN

Silence sleeps on sand.
Muted granules fragment
Between broken jetty stones
Salt water laps patterned poetry
Brooding in storm skies night.
Tides flow westerly greeting Alaskan currents
Shimmering twilight across phosphorescent
Restless
Heaving
Sea swells comforting land
Crooning Neptune's song.
This ocean only mutters to itself.

Strained ambitions surface.
Breakwater protects midnight solitude
Positioned on hard rock piles
Soul submerged in the action of waves
Slapping wet knees
Humming forgotten shanties
Sailors chant when lost at sea
Before the ship sinks.

Harbor lights guide calm clouds
Stitching stars on the needle
Of a new moon waking
Slivers of prophecy
Delivering thunder in whispers
To a sky of spangled pinpoints
Glowing bonfire checkpoints.

Beneath this transient
Armored shielded breast
Hand holding thunderstorms violent
Breath expels steaming vapor trails
Matching lub-dub drumming
Tattooed cadences of seas
Rising and falling whitecaps
Rising and falling heart beats
Rising and Falling breath
Comes the sigh of God
Whispering
This night passenger
Home.

No storm watch warnings
From any lighthouse in the vicinity
Hear prayers pleading.
Stillness starves the last campfire.

East on this Pacific rim
Sky blinks surprised
Cracks the night boundary
Sleepy
Yawning wide
Buttery morning stretches
Glides open
And then
Ahhhh then
Then
The Dawn God strides down
Burning mountains
Kissing me roundly on the mouth.

THE LAST CHURCH

Is this the last church before winter?
My wine does not turn into the blood of Christ.
My devotion is a bucket of holes.
My prayers are surgical procedures.
I have lost myself.
So you pray for me God
While I work out the bugs.
You pray for me God
Until I find my way again.

Is this the last church before winter?
My work hurts heavy
My style is tacky
My losses are grief
Sticky with reminders
There is a brine of dishonesty
Salted across these pages of tales
Uncertain
Words mean anything anymore.

Is this the last church before winter?
I abandon drawing water
From ancient desert wells
Chattering incessant trivial repetitions
Jabbering descriptions scolding gravestones
Determining lost causes of numbness
Drawing forth water from damaged sorrows.
I want my disappointments bravely bandaged
Confined with locally grown organic fences
Attractively planted with wild flowers
Smelling gilded gold
Arranged in silver sunlight expressions
Blossoming on the faces of my children.
If you pray for me God
I might recover.

INCANTATIONS UNDER GLASS

Voyages are longer now
Sailing love and unloving
Sea salted tears bearing broad smiles
Rinsed in contradictions.
Fingers worry the tiller
Cracked boat breaks
Steering foggy waters deviates
Rhyming spells
Oceans ebb and flow
Locates equilibrium in
Tide pools.

Sailing this odd marine movement
Tumbles me sand smothered smooth
Dried brown withered
Aged stranded seaweed
Abandoned on brackish beaches.
Seasons expose sealight
Roll, unroll, furl, unfurl spreading order
Sails luff, drooping low
Leaking faded possibilities
Heavenward
Radiating constellations
Retreat with unrequited interrogations.

Drifting empty in this small skin skiff
Rolling over and under turbulent waves
A storm rising sea heaves change
Resets compass headings
Assures relocations
Ascends forceful savage
Whitecaps foam widespread warnings.
I trim sails with rough rope
Rougher hands.

Riding hurricanes in faulty life boats
Paddling fierce escapes
Against capsizing
Overturned
A swollen refugee
Becalmed in doldrums
Sipping wanderlust in scalding tin cups
Burning blisters on bits and pieces
Cresting waves far too crookedly
Batten down sieved hatches
Against gales pelting floods
Twisting wind wild
Pushing me drowning in riptides
Pulling me grinning ashore
Marveling.

KISSING FROGS

I can lie about birthdays
If I choose
But this blunt skin
Is always truthful.
I never kiss frogs anymore
I never met a frog
Who was a Prince
But I have met a few Princes
Who were frogs once or twice.

Mother   never   told   me
Conversations would be reduced
Accompanied by whining itemizations
Summarizing causes of anesthetizing
When rules are delivered
In non-speaking envelopes
Scolding reminders of good conduct
Mailed by the silent sons of Kings.

Mother never told me
I would one day arrive
Locked in solitary confinement
Requiring body armor
Wishing any speeches mattered.
In the house sounds of silence
Lacerate behind closed doors.

I have frown creases now.
Laugh wrinkles tease
Crinkling renewable eye corners.
Somewhere above my kneecaps
Skin tilts downhill
Following gravity to the floor.
I am the meaning of
Necessary detachment
My urge to protest suppressed.

Shedding red cloaks of civil disobedience
Failing to salute properly
Failing to talk properly
Failing conversational prerequisites
Listed in dysfunctional books
I live in a novel
A story of a lost insurrections
Free speech vanquished
Vocabulary
Euthanized.

I fly a clean white flag of failed truces
Weary of wearing difficulties while others
Stand on my wings.

THE BELLY OF DRAGONS

With a fistful of anarchy rising
Your haughty expertise
Dominates the center of required attention
Theatrical dramas spoken in chaos.
Stirring pots
Spinning webs
Reclining in padded comfort
Sinking into fat pillows
Consuming self-admiring vapidities
Repeating memorized excuses
Taking leisure you uncork consequences
Toasting vanity with wine labeled
Conscientious Contrary Competence
Clinking a cracked mirror
Congratulating yourself.
Far away a chandelier tinkles.

Meanwhile
In the belly of dragons
My face spits out rebellious nonfiction
In Everest conditions
Of ill-fated expeditions suffocating slowly
Climbing uphill laddering over crevasses
Communicating the long unmoving
Goodbye.

PRESENTING MASKS

Don't see what you see.
Pretend the person facing me is not asleep.
Remember boundaries have mine fields.
Smile.
At appropriate times scream.
Study the difference.

Never reveal.
My body enclosing pure cosmos.
Do not share.
Inquiring is suicide do not ask.
Use slow movements.
Do not startle others.
Act as if private rotations around the sun
Will not burst into 92 million miles of star food
Lighting a whirling celestial planet
Solar steam bringing heated dawns
At all twenty-four hour revolutions.
Never expose small comets flashing heartseeds

Keep cautious secrets quiet while
Solar flares encircle
Welting skin twitches
From intermittent lost stars
Falling soul hardened
Reaching for God's breath.

Practice watchful wary
Daily weekly monthly yearly
Close encounters of the First Kind.
Use pre-programmed transmissions
Others comprehend
Translating pre-recorded meaning
Not at all mine.
Always carry duct tape in my pockets
A better first aid for wrong talk than lipstick.

Employ scripted speaking formulas in librettos.
Bank heaven's hell hot fires
Blazing out-of-control eruptions
Ecstasies being recovered
So others will not envy
My scorching glory
Eternal nebulas
Spinning trajectories of truth.

Wobble wounded in all discussions
In the DMZ of group collisions
Rehearse conversations played
Over and over and over
Learned from twittering answering machines
So others will not be envious of my
Dancing in primary colors
On the axis of conspicuous joy.

Pay no attention to people too busy to look up.
Act as if gods and goddesses do not whisper
Suggestions suppressing laughter
When I stumble off balance on broken scree
Navigating thin air angled mountains
High above tree line
Pretending I cannot fly\

PENANCE

Over the howl of lost years
Decades paying compound interest
Multiplied by 100,000 sleepless
Nights
Sinking
Into revisions
Morning skies startle
Awake
Haunted
My children's voices echo
Dreaming
Waking me
In strange places
With stranger recalls.
I counted all resemblances
Stored them in mason jars
Of contained amusement
Searching
Along amplified limits of space
Bottoms of canyons crumble
Calving glaciers shriek groans
Alpine snow winter dwellers shovel
Yellow aspen leaves fall
Boulders guard stream beds
Deserts inspire heat
Boots kick solitary dust motes
Hurry blue tailed lizards along.
Sometimes straining upward
Embracing night skies
Speaking constellations
Searching the North Star
Seeking Orion's Belt
Chasing celestial spheres
Longing for left-over welcomes.

Mornings always arrive on time.
Cold
Or hot
Or misty
Or snowy
Or rainy
Or just plain daylight
Always on time
Hard as cold oatmeal.

I looked for you
Marking prayerful additions with
Corrections.
It no longer matters
What morning looks like
After a night pleading my campaign
With heaven.

Eternities arrive
Beckoning free climbing explorations
Holding firm in parables
Angels listen.
You speak mediations.
I spent my coin on regrets
In the night
And
Here we go
Again.

PRAYER REQUEST

Prayers requesting God's presence
Don't seem to work.
I need to talk.
Prayers requesting God's attendance
Don't seem to work.
I need a quest.
Prayers requesting God's attention
Don't help me get up again.
Prayers requesting God's focus
Don't help me laugh.
Prayers requesting God's awareness
Don't keep me warm at night.
Prayers requesting God's interest
Don't help heal wounds.
I need to pray.
And can't find the inflection.
Holding hands in silence
Does not raise callouses
Nightmare hours lead me liquid
To your waters
Surrendering
At last.

IT IS NOT THAT

You ring the bell on my front porch
Beginning again your theater
My concrete steps a stage
Your tired tirade
A non-adapted speech older
Than wrinkles around my eyes.
(What are you talking about?)

It is not that.

You shout your enlightened duty is
Correcting my realities
Delivering a script on wickedness
Explaining jealousies unknowable
(What are you talking about?)

It is not that.

This spendthrift complaining
Bad breath pronouncing verbs
Shrilling sour sharp stern disapprovals
Ping hailstone sobs against windows.
(What are you talking about?)

It is not that.

It is not shouting toxic tall tales
Emailing hate snake utterances
As if they are prizes of
Lapis Lazuli
A gift no guru would give
Advising holy indictments
Of the way I am
(What are you talking about?)

Snap, zap, cobra strike of bone fingers
A cavalier arm sweep
Emphasizing a ledger of accusations
Requires immediate forced severance.

(What are you talking about?)

        It is not that.

It is not your imperious commands
Slapping me silly infected
With the syphilis of
Far Fetched grievances
Or your brilliant
Sylvia Plath brain
Shooting at me
From your bell jar
Of ungoverned over-excited dramas.
(What the hell are you ranting about?

        It is not that.

Please get a grip on your poor pitiful me.
Consult your Shaman.
Whimper "Am I not so right?"
Meanwhile get off my porch.
I don't know what the hell you howl about.

        What is it then?

Frankly, my dear, I don't give a damn

        You are not (shhhhhh)
        that important.

TRUCE

I lost my taste for justified rejections.
I am creaky scary old
Besotted with gravity
Skin cannot lie in the mirror
It takes courage to look
At this revolution of the body.

I have no yearning for princes
Who are frogs waiting to be kissed
Or white horses prancing
Nor burning witches
Nor climbing smooth glass mountains
With no traction
Exhausted when climbing up
Slipping in blood
When sliding down.

I am become mellow
Quiet
Less expectant
Curiously watching
Going down more than up
Falling
Breaking
With frequency.
There are no more infernos
Blistering this aching beingness
Nailing my soul shut.
The dogs are allowed
To nap on the couch
Finally.

I am learning acceptance
What is parceled out
In measured packages
Delivered only when my soul
Can afford the stamps
Or someone looks up from the cell phone.

I am learning to settle for rare moments
Surprised discovering wisdom
Rebellions mollified
Surrendering
I've learned the cruelest thing
Isn't leaving
It's coming back.

SITTING ON CURBS

Dogs die
Waiting for people.
People never die
Waiting for a dog.

Unlike dogs
We want it all.
We petition wishes with flourishes
Land grants from the King
Feathered arrows killing hearts
Obedience
Tolerance for tantrums
Influence
Money
Cruelty
We tell God what to pray for us.
His silence disappoints.

What we really desire is
Everything.
Refusing responsibility
We corrupt biology
Avoiding
Laws of entropy
  (Women are tasked clean-up
    Of bloodstained random messes
      Don't you know that yet?
       The dogs know it.)
We want it all.

While sitting on curbs in underwear
We don't want clothes.
We don't want shelter.
We want it all.
E-V-E-R-Y-T-H-I-N-G

       (our way

             Unlike appreciative dogs)

We don't respect loyalty
Or a little starvation
Or an offer of salvation
We pant open mouthed
Wanting more
Everything.

EMPTY ME

How can I ever speak again?
I am unlicensed
To fly like this.

How can my spinning hawk soul
Soar hungry in pure skies
With white doves
When this beak violently eats
My transgressions bloody
In daily absolutions.

My only reference points
Tighten transgressions
Against amnesty
Against the rules of gravity
Against pardons
Tame fierce thrashing growling
Desires
Longing to ask
To answer
And be at last
Fully empty.

WHO LIVES IN THIS SKIN?

Wind is always forward movement.
The inward stretch crossing water.
Do you hear bombastic conversations
Between surf and land?
Wind sweeps skies across river banks
Seeks toes walking on water gripping
Wails bagpipe whistles
Pushes land-grasses moaning long notes
Against bare legs
Knocks fences down
Croons lullabies
Cradles an ocean slumbering
Rejoices flinging water on beaches
Rattles tides breaking
Every hard edge

      Into sand
            Into sand
                  Into sand through the hourglass
FALLING DOWN
To the work of pulping rock
Digging canyons
Smoothing sandstone cliff faces
Slowly carving glorious monuments
      Of sand
            Of sand
                 Of sand through the hourglass

FALLING DOWN
Collecting particles of recognition
Commenting on intervals
Becoming invisible
Separating elements
Measuring accuracy
Nearly almost invisible
Only flecks of what remains behind
When wind unwinds me small.
The calculating hourly globe inverts
Reveals storms of situations
Confused sorrows of lamentations
Stilled conversations hands stifle
Once hard thrown
          Of sand
                    Of sand
                              Of sand through the hourglass
FALLING DOWN
Against the rise of the sun
Sky gazing the Evening Star
Leans in curved spaces between
Forward movements of syllables
          Of my sand
                    Of my sand
                              Of my sand through the hourglass
FALLING DOWN
I know you
Inside deep pockets
Where I live behind my eyes.
I cannot touch
Your arrogance
Or the immensity of the downpour
When shoveling mad sandy exits
Seasoning my waters with tornadoes
Rounding up cows jumping over the moon
And pigs flying.

I attend carefully poised
Patrolling interference your
Guarded perimeter constructs
In the morning debris of nursery rhymes.
I am rainstorms blown sideways
        Into sand
                Into sand
                        Into sand
FALLING DOWN
        Into my sand through the hourglass.

TO ——————— WITH LOVE

Oh!
The blistered mortar shell
Struck
And struck
And struck
And struck
Until you were a sieve
They could pour a jungle through.

You came home wordless.
Silver jet wings singing your obituary
Dressed for a formal
Occasion
In black rubber
Your mama cried
I remember.
We clenched our fists
Feeling helpless.

Your name is spun
Final
In satin letters
On a black slab in Washington DC
Arms are empty that
Would hold you
Until morning.

I saw her with one red rose.
She was dressed in a book
Of poems.
Your coffin wore
Red thoughts
From your red blood
And red lovings
Now undone
Bent her to her knees.
We wept.

1969 Vietnam
You had to be there with us.

BENEATH JUNGLE FOLDS

I think of Joe Lacey
Turning slowly
Into Asian mud
Beneath the jungle folds
Of green baboo carpet
In Vietnam.

Joe left two orphans
A boy...
A girl...
A wife thirty pounds overweight
From easing her grief
In the peanut butter jar.

I think of Joe Lacey
His tank flickering flames
Scorching twisted metal fragments
Steaming him to death
Then a tidy telegram to Honolulu.
Two orphans...
A widow.

I cradled his infant son
Ate spaghetti with his new bride
We mused about war until sunrise
Drinking nervous
Laughing false
Held fast together relying on
These youthful
Dreams.

We watched a marathon of men
Invade Canada.
People stopped speaking
Defecting north at 110 mph
On highway 89
When the state of things summoned
Conscription lottery invitations
Arriving in virgin mailboxes.
You are ordered. Surprise\

It was dangerous to be
Young and strong and male.
Later years purchased
Amnesty for bolting.
Those boys picked up bags
Government gratuities
And moved back home.

Other Mothers sons
Living in bunkers
Shouting "Incoming"
Dodged RPGs.
Emptied of everything.
Drained young strong warriors
Paid the Piper's bride price
Waiting for something bad to happen
Returned to foreign hometowns
Stepped jet lagged
Over-dressed in GI green
Carrying terrified medals in dufflebags
Homesick
Confused
Homecoming worse
Than jungle ambushes.
Or they arrived home in rubber bags.
Or stood lined up
At unemployment offices
Brushing away spit and garbage

Wounded again overwhelmed by
Righteous peaceful citizens
No More War brutally throwing trash
Bombing with garbage and spiteful spit
Barely survived sons and daughters.

Burning flags
Nation wrenching
Peaceful? hate and blame protests
Chanting
Hissing
Spitting
Peace? marchers violent
Militant
Strutting viciously coy
A charade of nonviolent mocking
Attacking wounded souls.

I think of Joe Lacey
Who was my friend
Gasping in seared pieces
Smearing great satin blood stains
Across dew-bright morning grasses
Trailing orphans and a widow
In glistening reddening puddles
Of dying far from home.
His charred grim flesh
Paid blood prices.
Now we listen to complaining
Safe people shouting ignorance again
Sniping from sanctimonious distance
Far away from blood loss
Thinking they are free.

Joe Lacey's legacy?
Two orphans
A boy.
A girl.
A notification officer
A folded flag
A widow in Honolulu
Easing grief
In a peanut butter jar

BATTLE BLOOD

Battle blood invades the senses
Weaving, cleaving,
Grieving, seeing
Leaving all defenses open
Cast in chaos unprotected
Groping in the darkening threat
Flanked by other silhouettes
Probing in the fading dimness
Sprinting forward eyes in grimness
Knowing there is no relief.
Reality intermingles
Trapping, clutching
Tearing, beating
Hearts and souls in desperate weeping
Vessels broken no repair
Waiting for the Huey's care.
Coming home is full of sorrow
Wounds and memories wake tomorrow
Left alone in startled memory
Empty, shredded never remedy.

BYSTANDER

Ho Chi Minh
A greater sin
Agent Orange.
Huey's hover
Jungle cover
Dust off needy
Help is speedy
Death is greedy.
Land them
Kill them
Bring them home
Damaged broken to the bone
Go Crazy.

Special Forces
Skill endorses.
Westmoreland.
Hell No We Won't Go
Khe Sahn pinned down
What the hell
I'm gonna drown.

Iron Triangle
Search destroy
ChuChi tunnel hell deploys.
DMZ, M16, Napalm, Punji sticks
A Nation's young the only pick.
The most disturbing things they see
Include snipers in the trees.

Draft Dodgers
Canada
My Lai Oh My!
Kent State
We will not participate

Kissinger and Kennedy
Johnson lost in reverie
Peace with Honor
Bet my ass
All our allies shot at last.
MIA POW
Lay to rest all the sorrow
On marble's memory for tomorrow.

MEDALS OF HONOR
with all due respect

I am the pace of dying
Running from itself
With more courage than fear.
Who can make scratches
Of permanence
In a flag draped steel coffin?
I am become
The posthumous memory you dread
Preserved forever
In proud pride
I am a blue ribboned medal
Under glass
In a frame
On a mantel of tears.
Of course all I wished of war
Was coming home to you.

EAST OF RAMAGEN

He never talked much about The War.
When we asked, jumping up and down
At his feet,
"What did you do in the war, Daddy?"
He shrugged big shoulders
And changed the subject.

He told us once
Of children with wan war faces.
Skinny German kids
With eyes big in small bodies.
Children too busy starving for games
Wandered GI encampments
Rummaged trash heaps
Searched for something to eat.
He told us this over breakfast one morning
When we wouldn't finish our eggs.
Ragged war waifs seeking food
Waited for GI finished meals
Then quick with rodent skills
Urgent raided garbage barrels.
Military waste furnished feasts
When anything would do to eat.

That was all we were told
When we were small and growing-up
Over half of western America
Singing songs, traveling highways
In his shiny, grey, custom-ordered Buick,
Looking out windows at corn fields passing
Our bellies full of hamburgers and French fries.

When I was grown
We stayed up late
When I came home to visit,
We talked and joked
After Mother climbed the stairs to bed
He'd get out the scotch and milk
Delivering kitchen dissertations
At the sink-board lectern.
We would try speaking of things
So close and hard
As friends do
When they talk late into night
With lamps on low.

One night we spoke of the dog.
Put to sleep after fourteen years
Kids still cried months later
Blessing her in every small evening
Liturgy of prayer
At bedsides
Small voices in hard mourning.
We talked of death and dying
What it means to children
What it doesn't mean to grown-ups.
He, with his scotch and milk
I, listening.
With halted speech
His story started
Like the old car stalling on frostbitten
Montana winter mornings.
Words coming slow
Then in staccato bursts.
How German Panzers were beautiful
Dark angels beckoning death.
How narve soldiers laid rifles down
Going into trees
Along the shell shocked road
Taking leaks

Never thinking they might leave their souls
Spattered on tree trunks.

It was the Battle of the Bulge
I never learned in history books.
Some crazy, mixed-up offensive
East of Ramagen
When enemies changed all the road signs.
No one who cowboyed in the West
Knew where they were
Some said later
Even who they were
He was twenty-one or twenty-two
I forget his years.
Young.
Driving a dynamite truck
He stopped
Waiting for rumbling war machines
Chasing combat.
He saw a jeep
The usual bruised army green
Towing a large wagon
Hurrying
Dodging mortar fire
On a bomb fractured road.
Stopping along his ammo truck.
He saw.
He saw.
He saw the wagon contents.
Bodies
Tossed together.
A flaunting
War ruined display
American's young
Bloody, bruised, fractured, broken
Bouncing in a wagon
Wrecked beyond repair.

He saw.
He saw.
Death's crushed cargo
Bumping on a rutted battle road
Somewhere in Belgium or Germany
No one knew where.
He learned Death
Before their mother's knew.

Legs and arms embracing
Crumpled faces
Grimacing in unexpected boldness.
Death the devil's payment
Cloaked in spreading blood stains
The uniform of the day.
Mother's sons war tangled
In tired boots
Damaged, cracked, sole-less
Frostbitten toes blackened
By endless weary European marches
In bitter winter's 1944 freezing ditches.
Emptied soldiers swayed together piled
A broken pulse of bafflement
In a jeep heap of violent waste.
Serrated lifeless young
All surprised.
All squandered witnesses
In a wagon of ruin
Purpose and desire finished.

At twenty-one or two
He hung gaping
Over the steering wheel
Of a dynamite truck
Somewhere in Belgium or Germany
No one knew where
Staring at scorched earth's harvest
His blasted brain
Shocked in battle fire and smoke.

In a faraway kitchen
Forty years later
With a scotch to give him words
And I hope, a daughter
Giving him faith,
He buried his head in his hands
And wept.
After forty years my father wept.

1945. Germany. WWll . Dad

ICARUS

Soundless
Miles above the sea
A glorious seeking of
Bronze heat hot beating gold
His heart
Hushed the upward stretching
For the fires of heaven
Then
The rushing roar
Arms flung wild
Enfolding wind
Feet dangling
Frenzied prayers
Flapping hands
The spiral terror of gravity
Feathers on waves
Softly drowning.

GUINEVERE

I know Guinevere
Who lies
Between red silk cushions
Meditating
Unthinkable agencies
    One within the Right hand
     One within the Left hand
     Waiting
As dawn stoops old
Over day grey dull hills
In Camelot.

I know Guinevere
Who lies
Heavy caught
Between guarded choices
Breast burning crimson
    One within the Right
     One within the Left
     Waiting
As noon day burns
Field bright hilltops
In Camelot

I know Guinevere
Who lies
Between imprisoned longings
Heart tolling somber silver bells
Questing near cold stone
    One within the
     One within the
     Waiting
As sky fairies whisper
On moon-shredded high summits
In Camelot.

I know Guinevere

Who lies
Between dreams
In pale sleeplessness
Staring, aching
          One within
              One within
                  Waiting
As midnight death
Pours savage across
Blood ruined fields
In Camelot.

I know Guinevere
Who lies between two
          One
              One
                  Waiting

GILES COREY'S LEGACY

Where beneath green softness
Lying down with
Angel's broken wings
Peeps the cobweb of the sky
Pressing Giles Corey's bones
In broken rhythm crushing down
Stones immense in valued continuity
Smothering in azure agonies
Prodigal theft
The village church
Billowed bulges cracking wide
Symmetry in layered vengeance
Swirling round and round.
Leave all thought of wringing hands
Or drying tears lovers.
More weight. More weight!
Give me more weight!
I seek the soil to lie alone
An evacuee from ludicrous
Christianity.

1692. Salem, Massachusetts

THOUGHTS ON A WINTER'S TALE

I read you William Shakespeare.
I read the taste of your skin
Salting the page
Knowing no biography
I read You old man
Hunched
Grey
Fingers thin
Emptying pages of yourself
Pulling at tattered ragged
End-pieces of cynicism
Like one quietly
Pulls out
Hair.

I read you
Wet tears between lines
Knowing your life's wintering
In dark December's bitter parchment.
Clothes thinning
Blood thinning
Love thinning
Poetry thinning
Ink thinning
Thoughts thinning
A blizzard of emptiness.

Is your pen like you now?
Snowbound
Hollowed out by storms
Making chilled observations
About disappointing people
Darkly inking
Another page preserving
Conversations?
Are cadavers the remains

In your closet?
I read you wondering.
Do you smell daffodils
Hearing a shepherd chant
As you write
One final punctuation mark of endings?

Do you desire spring
One more time before
Fingers on the frosty hourglass
Spin your soul's dry conclusions
In cold forever seasons
Where fame's fires
Provide little warming
In hungry darkness.

In the withered rue
Of dry virility
I read your desire.
Do you long to hold her wrinkled breast
Lying warm one last moment?
Do you smell thoughts of
Sweat on the back of her knees
Drowning in folds of her skin
Pushing her taste against your teeth
Eavesdropping groans
In the back of her fevered throat
Wrapped one last time
In the sun of youth
Warm in her embrace
Dazzled
While love never-minds all losses
In between?

I read you, William Shakespeare
Tired
Sighing jaded
Leaning heavy in candlelight
Greying
Weary with words
And paper
And pens
And actors
And globed audiences.

I read your
Waiting
Applause dying
Conversations waning
Behind the closing curtain.

GANGES RIVER

Lost beyond losing.
Found beyond finding.
The endless eye of God
Burns this pyre of willing bones
These stone-bones
These bleached in the sun, stark raving mad bones
These slashed scattered bones
These calcified branches bones,
These food for roots and small grubbing things bones.
These blanched, cleaved, stripped, ripped bones.
Burns bones into beaches
Wind washed land stoops
Above continental plates moving fast
Beneath stumbling tides.
Burns falling into ocean's bones
Collapsing stone opus bones
Transformed speckled, freckled, dotted, stippled
Drifting airborne ash bones
Gone billowing upward in the thinnest of breezes
Ash.

Ash pouring heat into this sacred turquoise
Shining Holy River of gossamer eons
Watered in the eternal smile of God.
This star-stone anointed bone heart shudders
Stutters, stops, inhales,
Gathers human existence
Breathing inferno ash thoughts
Exhaling flying ash dying thoughts
Drying in the hot sun ash thoughts,
Funeral pyre rocketing red-hot ash skyward
Ash falling backward into river mud.

This ash mouth inhaling
Exhaling dappled, smoldering ruin thoughts
These fired ash-dared choruses
Mortal mouths thoughts
These blazing, stinging, suffocating, singing,
Alarming thoughts
These merging into galaxies hurrying to heaven
Stars-on-fire thoughts.
Flinging all this burning, pyre, bonfire, ashes to ashes
Spectacle
Into starry night, start-again, don't stop, forever after
Draperies of moving, holy, watered, gravel, sand, mud
Ash
Turquoise river flowing steady with no-never-mind
Into endless God.

I am stone cleaved.
I am stone annulled.
I am stone become wood.
Wood become pyre.
Pyre become spark.
Spark become flame.
Flame become moonlight.
Moonlight falling, falling, falling
Ash-light, ash-bright
Weighty with insignificance
Freckled, glowing, flickering, hot terminated
Ash.

I am stone-bone tears.
I am stone-bone heart.
I am stone-bone suns of fire
Inhaling exhaling
Panting bits of smoldering ash
Folded in the
Flaming shawl of God.

I am ash.
A speckle of diamonds
Tossed across water
This hot ash mouth
Pushes out breath
Grinding rock to gravel
Gravel to sand,
Sand to Holy Turquoise River
Holy Turquoise River gliding to God.

I am joyous ash weeping in hot skin.
I am weeping ash ignited by empty suffrage.
I am singing ash tasting honey
I am ash answering God's kiss.
I am ash answering answering answering,
Smashing through flesh
Ascending the starry sky.

I Am
Ash
Bearing gifts
Toward Oceans kept Holy
In a single tear.

*Beside the Ganges in India
You should have been there me*

NOTES TO MY CHILDREN

I should be wise
Maybe
Perhaps
Why
God knows I am old enough
To sit down hard
With sages of ages
When people are judged
Clever
Astute
Compliant
Or dumber than rocks on a sidewalk.
I should
At the very least
Be moderate
Residing fragile
Kept within all restricted
Group approved patterns
Who made these arrangements?

I definitely should avoid
Avoid
Political conversations
Indefinitely
(Of course I'll be arrested
Without habeas corpus)
Who approved this sameness?

I should be
Old enough
Wise enough
Shrewd enough
Not to expose myself
For one single stuttering heartbeat
Between gasps.
I should damn well be concerned
With obsessions of others.
Hair style. Check.
Italian vegan shoes. Check.
Latest household robots. Check.
Advocating tents on sidewalks
For the homeless. Check.
Facebook self-promotion page. Check

Note to my children.
There is no wind in plagiarized
Xeroxed similar paper sails.
There is no beach in Toe the Line.
There is no soaring sky kiting
In shocking counterfeit think alike
Corrupted imagination
Contaminated colors
Do not color outside the lines
Mandates scary people demand.
Who dreams up this cloning legislation?

Please remember
Treaties are forthrightly
Immediately
Forgotten
Abruptly terminated
Without notice
When gold is discovered in the Black Hills.
Beware of treaties
Hide the gold.
Who ordered treaties anyway?

On this particularly impressive afternoon
Writing this missive in my head
Driving Red Mountain pass
Unintimidated
Held close on curves precipitous
Overhanging the Gorge
Celebrating shapes in the sky
Smiling with raucous remembrance
I love arm wrestling this road
Numerous points of view descend
This steep chasm.
Downshifting mountain curves fast
Eagerly barefoot in gravel
Scarves twirling in primary colors
Sleeping beloved by the river
With the door open
There is plenty of peace
To go around.
Come and take me.

Today a wee bit of
Admiration will be nice
On a mountain grove picnic
Sponsored by champagne celebrations.
Too much to ask?
OK. Back to rowdy.
Dangerous mountain passes are
Interesting
Don't miss them.

Life is a painful tight corset squeeze
In the trenches of sameness
Meaning is removed by Watchers
Penning shameless oversight regulations.
Who requires these social masks?

Ask yourselves.
What do Watchers know?
These plump unschooled sausages
Voyeurs smothering imagination
Bliss
Harmony
Ecstasy
Organizing holy correctness scripture
Stifling curiosity 613 threads at a time.
Who are these smothering regulators?
Who desires required apparel?
Who wishes uniformed thought advice?
Who demands no conversations?

Be brave my young ones.
Avoid those refusing barefoot travel
Along edges of muddy small ponds
Perfect goo sticking between toes
Dirty feet silly amused messy.
Avoid the contaminated intentions of
Pattern builders, supervisors, managers,
Bosses, peers, spouses,
Friends, mothers-in-law
Imposing etiquette for use of white tablecloths
Throw away the table cloth.

Who are these people
Standing on your wings?

Go boldly forward happy shoeless.
Stay in your pajamas all day.
Film your own movie.
Be the eagle flying borders of purpose
Over ridges of Wind River mountain snows.
Hunting.

CURIOUS CUSTOMS

I am winter wet mountains
Melting
Unrestricted snow
Learning white water
Consorting with boulders
Watering wild flowers
Hurrying to the sea.

I am clouds
Hanging Tibetan prayer flags
Flying sky colors
On the gathering darkness
Of the deepening gale.

I am green sea
Writhing anarchy
Browsing chaos
Along the pillars
Of the bottomless shore.
I am tangled webs of
Silk dreamed curiosity
Dissolving in impossibility.

I am fear barking at the moon
In night hours
Suffering from snake bite.
I am a heart of abstractions
Logic stifled
By transforming my religions.

I am a building on fire.
I am terrifying passion
Dancing circles and squares
On frontiers of deliverance.

I am a silent revolution
Speech has stopped.
I am a festival of light
A cheering parade
Going to a funeral.

I am no beggar
No passenger
No poet
No guest
Not even a prospective
Carnival barker.

I am not your enemy.
I am standing against the wall
With a machine gun pointed
At my gut
Holding my breath
In disconcerted surprise.

THIS CHURCH?

In this Church
Which I do not attend
In this confessional
Where I do not participate
Or wave the banners of
My sins talking loudly
Or light holy candles
Begging for something
On bleeding knees
I ask a Priest
Behind a screen
Covering his eyes
With a shameless hand
Who is the Patron Saint of
Remorse and Regret?
I hear his eyes crinkle
Lips curling upward
The chuckle forming
Silent
At the corners of his mouth.
A cough.
Why
He says
You are.

EXPATRIATE

Sun-seared
Sweat-soaked
Skin-pitted
I woke on the beach
Of desolations.
Sky-sneered
Sea-pulsed
Wind-tasted
Star-shod
With all of my Selves.
Your arrow sang flight
Hell-hot and heavy.
This wordless heart burst
A blood of noise
Evacuating.
The walls of sunset
Graved me.

7

Seven decades
Become a rusty latch
Pushing
Cracked wood gate whining
Open.
Dust covered boots
Weary on hills
Unsteady in fields
Easing forward with stiffening joints
Aging ferocious.

No coward hides here
Behind
Words
Disillusioned.
I mark my passage
Leaving a flagged tale of
A woman's misadventures
Apologizing for anguish.

I loved you.

No one survives the sack of a city.

Old women value black snowflakes
Walking north in crushing ruin
Lean hard against polar silence
Where we rise
Speaking out loud
And sit down again
In winter.
Cold.

MY RIVER SONG

I am your foreigner
A sorceress of curiosity
All this peculiar lifetime
Standing
Falling
Swimming
Flailing
Riding
Bobbing along
Fast currents in white-water
Pushing hard against
Ribs of my soul
Dancing me forward
To the sea
Foaming
Sparkling
Striking against rocks
Leaping spray
Spinning whirlpools
Floating eddies
Drowning deep water
Walking shallows
Moving swift
Resting slow
Moving not in the least.
Liquid river washing shorelines
Hurrying to the Sea.
This is my river.
This is the river of me.

White water cascades
Chills skin blue
Goose bumps
Licking sky tastes
In the sweat of river life.

Earth recycles me
In rotations
Of night and day
Seasons sway
Sashaying through evaporated moments
The way a woman twitches
Her hips in colored skirts
Turning into clouds.

Meadows glitter silver flower lace
Forest loamy smells
Passing in the night
Spring run-off
Silver salmon flash near stone waterfalls
And my river keeps running downhill
Running fast
Running free
In musical demented joy
Downhill.
To the sea.
I have been standing
All my life
Kissed
By this river
By this sea urgent hurrying
Chanting God songs
Tasting salt sandy
On the tip of my tongue
Corroding the edges of my bones
Running downhill
River.

Finding footing
Singing slippery mud banks
Wobbly wearing out wet to the soul
Song of rivers washing me
Quick silvered elusive.
Shivering in airborne droplets
Making haste
Moving on downhill
The seaward side of marshland
Whistles me home
Where birds startle winging west
Into sunset.

I am running rapids
On a white water calliope
Flowing harmony down canyons
Surging gravity
Water dancing the spine of the world
Flooding rotations of earth
Falling through day and night
Rocketing to sun and moon
Splashing into spray
Going to the sea.
Going in this river
To the sea.
Going home.

VIGNETTE VIII

Swimming in this odd Ocean

I am become

Tumbled smooth

Dried brown

Aged like stranded seaweed

On the salt beach.

And one by one the nights between our separated stars are joined

to the arc of the sky.

Thank You Pablo Neruda

TKW

About the Author

Williams began rhyming poems sitting on her poet grandmother's lap in Rocky Mountain thunderstorms. A lifetime of writing and reading feeds her challenge of merging vivid imagery with shifting human desires.

She has master's degrees in communication, theater, and cultural anthropology. Her children, grandchildren, horses, dogs, mountains and the embrace of the sea are her teachers and playground. She is the child of the great American western panorama and the lure of crisscrossing a country on long lonely roads, the hum of tires her song.

CONVERSATIONS is unapologetic with immediate resonance, familiarity and frank honesty. Making skillful connections of language with the rhythms of sound and imagery, she plants seeds of realization with a directness we often hide.

Read aloud, her stanzas gain momentum, flipping over other possibilities and new meanings as she journeys through the fierce gift of wisdom living delivers.

She isn't hiding her world. She is having a painted conversation.